# Search for the Sacred:

## The New Spiritual Quest

# Search for the Sacred:

## The New Spiritual Quest

*edited by*
*Myron B. Bloy, Jr.*

 THE SEABURY PRESS · NEW YORK

ACKNOWLEDGMENT

Grateful acknowledgment is made to the following authors and publishers for permission to use copyrighted material from the sources listed:

Doubleday and Company—Delmore Schwartz, *Summer Knowledge*: New and Selected Poems 1938–58. Copyright 1959 by Delmore Schwartz.

Alfred A. Knopf, Inc.—Wallace Stevens, "Sunday Morning," *Collected Poems, 1955*. Copyright 1923, copyright renewed 1951, by Wallace Stevens.

The Macmillan Company—*Collected Poems of William Butler Yeats*. Copyright renewed 1952 and 1961 by Bertha Georgie Yeats.

*New Yorker* Magazine—Phillis Harris, "Furniture." Copyright © 1968 by New Yorker Magazine, Inc.

# CONTRIBUTORS

Robert N. Bellah
*Professor of Sociology*
*University of California*

Betsy Brenneman
*Denison University, '71*

Daniel Burke
*Chaplain to the Medical Center*
*University of Michigan*

James Forest
*Emmaus House, New York City*

Nancy Willard Lindbloom
*Poet and Professor of English Literature*
*Vassar College*

Stanley Newman
*Director, Uptown Peoples–Northeastern Illinois*
*University Center, Chicago*

Thomas Phelan
*Resident Catholic Chaplain*
*Rensselaer Polytechnic Institute*

Wayne Proudfoot
*Professor of Religion, Fordham University*

Caroline Kerman Schrag, *Non-Violence Trainer, and*
James L. Schrag, *Social Change Teacher*
*and Non-Violence Trainer, Philadelphia*

Richard A. Underwood
*Associate Professor of Philosophy of Religion*
*Hartford Seminary Foundation*

Austin Warren
*Professor Emeritus of English*
*University of Michigan*

Joan Webber
*Professor of English Literature*
*The Ohio State University*

Richard L. York
*Berkeley Free Church*

# Contents

## Part III: Confronting the "Sacred Yes"

# Search for the Sacred:

## The New Spiritual Quest

# Editor's Introduction

The Church Society invitation to participate in the consultation which produced these papers included the following warrant for and description of the task:

That there *is* a growing spiritual quest—especially, but not only, among the young—seems increasingly obvious. We see it overtly in the popularity of religious books, courses, and public lectures. Every religion known to man is being openly practiced in Cambridge and other academic centers today, and the music of Dylan, Harrison, Lennon, and Guthrie is laced with religious concern. This quest is also an implicit part of many overtly political actions, *e.g.,* the ritual and ceremonial aspects of the demonstration. In fact, whether because of the threat of chaos or the hope for larger life, many of the young have broken through the once self-sufficient technocratic world-view to the perception that life is rooted in mystery. Our consultation will focus on two questions, one analytic and the other strategic, in relation to this phenomenon: *What is the cause, present shape, and probable future of this quest? How should the Church—especially on the campus—relate to it?*

Those who participated in the consultation shared both a sensitivity to the spiritual dimension of reality and an awareness of the new spiritual quest currently taking place, but beyond that we were a widely diverse group, representing every part of the country: twenty-year-olds and seventy-year-olds; freaks and straights; students, faculty, and campus ministers; activists and contemplatives, of spiritual persuasions running the gamut from orthodox Christian to acid visionary. We gathered to test and deepen each other's perceptions for five days at the Narragansett Inn on Block Island at the head of Long Island

Sound. We chose this meeting site for several reasons: we felt that the remoteness of the island inn would provide the elbow-room and encourage the concentration our task demanded; we counted on the mysterious beauty of the sea island to inspire and refresh us for our work; and, finally, we could include William Stringfellow's considerable gifts in our consultation only by holding it on the island he was too ill to leave.

This book demonstrates the shape and thrust of our thinking and discussion. We were soon to discover that although the new quest was multifaceted, certain overall concerns and themes developed, and we have grouped together here, where appropriate, the responses of the participants to one or several of these thematic concerns so that the reader may experience in his own exploration the dialectic interplay of the participants' approaches and thinking. One aspect of the new quest—namely, what has come to be called the Jesus movement—is not covered here, largely because this aspect of the new quest has been treated in great detail elsewhere and also because we wanted to explore in greater depth other less well-known aspects.

On the whole, the responses of the participants cover not only essential background material and analyses; they also offer analysis and speculative assessment in a daring way of a phenomenon which is not only various but also at the present time shifting, tentative, and groping for shape in some of its significant manifestations. Still other responses bring us up short before the earthiness and hard realities which some questers are encountering.

Another dimension of the consultation, and one revealed only by implication in the responses, is the spirit of community which began to emerge among the participants as we struggled to grasp the nature of the current spiritual search—and of our own experience. For, despite the fact that our diversity of experience and assumptions became at times a centrifugal, and almost disabling, force, it finally led for most to an awareness of the deeper ground on which unity in diversity could be achieved.

There were three such moments of a "growing in grace" for the community Austin Warren came to call "the church at Block Island," "the saints gathered at the Narragansett Inn." One such moment took place at a gathering at Eschaton, the bluff-edged home of William Stringfellow and Anthony Towne; the second at a luncheon with a number of island citizens at Smuggler's Cove, where we were guests of the hospitable proprietor, Bengt Nordberg.

The third formative moment occurred when we received the news that Daniel Berrigan had fallen suddenly and seriously ill in prison. On that occasion James Forest read to us this portion of a letter he had received from the imprisoned Berrigan:

No point in mourning. Though I did myself at first. It is dreadful that good friends suffer. But how else will anything get accomplished? We have had years and years trying to find just that other way. And then it came to this. Now my feeling is that if we ever entertain regrets it will be because we did not take it in the neck earlier. But better late than not at all.

Of course we miss you. But in war people are always separated—and unarmed and killed. And we learn to bear with it. The worst has by no means happened to us—we are clothed and fed and have books, time, freedom to pray. The little we are asked to endure would be considered good fortune by millions of the world's poor. It is in that spirit we try to go forward, to hearten our friends. Certainly for priests and nuns to be jailed is an honor in such days—it will be one of the few honors the Church can point to in the years ahead. And we are honored to know and love them.

After a period of silence, Thomas Phelan led us in this prayer:

Father, the freedom of Daniel Berrigan looms large in the recent history of this island. It was here that he lost his freedom of action. But it was also here that in the very act of losing freedom of action, he asserted for all the world to see his inner freedom, the freedom of his mind and spirit. Handcuffs and dead-serious guards did not prevent his great smile and the gesture of peace, the old victory symbol. If it be your will, Father, to limit Dan's freedom of action further by grave illness, touch also his mind with greater peace and his spirit with fuller freedom. We pray this in the name of Jesus, our liberator. Amen.

While "the saints gathered at the Narragansett Inn" have long since dispersed, the fruits of their reflection and search have been brought together here for others to share—and to evaluate in the light of their own experience. One assurance that sustained us in our effort and that sustains an ever-growing number of searchers of the Spirit is Jesus' great word: "Ask and it will be given to you; search, and you will find; knock, and the door will be opened to you" (Matt. 7:7, JB).

In the pages that follow, the discussions and reflections of the participants have been grouped around three major themes: The Loss of Direction; the Quest for Direction; and Confronting the "Sacred Yes." Some participants, it will be noted, focused their major attention on only one or two of the themes.

N.B. The poem quoted serially on the part titles is "Climbing Mount Bross, August 1970" by Joan Webber.

# I

## The Loss of Direction

Hard rain and clouds sealed off the ravaged peaks.
The car's wheels spun in the mud, and I stayed the
    night
There, near the end of the road, excited, tense.
At five, in the dark, now under fading stars,
I sloshed through spongy bog to a mountain's base
And started blind, unsure which peak was which.

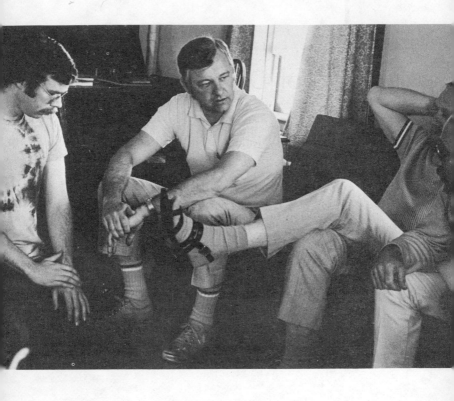

BETSY BRENNEMAN:

## The Way It Happened

Last year, in early winter, I felt the cosmos tip to me. Like a tremendous plastic bowl, it tilted suddenly, the rim fell past my eyes and the smooth crater dipped wide and deep below. Then, instantly righting itself, the edge rose up to its usual position above my head. I was not stoned. Although I cannot now recall the look of the crater, my life is inextricably bound to that second of movement when, frozen, I knew what was happening. I understood and I believed then that "human" meant soul.

Several months later, I was invited to Block Island to talk about spirit, youth, identity, and humanness; and as I was the youngest member of the group, it was hoped that I and the other student member would speak of feelings and events that could serve as the unrefined resource of our discussions. So I offer here a large part of myself and a little of my fellow youths. I have chosen to tell you first from where we came, then of the climax of my young spiritual life.

I am barely twenty-two. My mind—and the minds of millions like me—was molded by the middle-class values upon which my country thrived. Pulled into the greatest public school system the world had known, didn't we pour in? The postwar optimism that gilded the air at the moment of our conception shone from young parents' faces and reflected off ours as we gleamed our way through the blissful fifties and early sixties. With programmed math and field trips, questions were few and answers were plentiful. Pushed and tantalized by rewards that meant something real only to our parents, we were given the time, the money, and the mobility to try everything because "What a wonderful opportunity, dear!" it was. Those who were quicker and brighter earned their merit badges sooner, finding that approval from home gave them stronger spines and provided the only meaning and reason necessary. The "How To Be Popular" books kept appearing under the Christmas tree and the only demand was, "Just so you appreciate this." We were loved dearly.

Our hearts were shaped in warm stability. They beat in a shelter so total that they became elitists. We poured our affections on dead robins, Easter baskets, stuffed animals, and the student council election and we cheerleadered and Sunday schooled our way to easy ethics. Learning a new piano piece, the books of the Bible, or the school song all earned gold stars. There were D.A.R. medals for essays on the meaning of American history and shiny trophies for the Little League champs. The sense of well-being and warmth became confused only at rare moments when we learned that the little old man at the corner store was not to hug us in that way anymore.

Jackie Gleason screamed at Alice every Saturday night, Edward R. Murrow continued to talk to famous living rooms, and Jimmie and Roy ceaselessly asked the Mouskateers what time it was. Alan Shepard gave us TV in the classroom, and the school intercom told me my news for the day. I saw stainless steel replace our white kitchen sink and new additions stuck onto every school I attended. Eisenhower defeated Stevenson and I believed that one man was the president forever. Einstein and Schweitzer were my heroes, and *Science in Your Own Backyard* was my favorite book until I discovered the prowess of Nancy Drew and nonstop radio.

It all paid off. The stars of the middle class began to rise. The sweat off great-grandpa's immigrant brow was being redeemed by true Americanization, and all the time we were running on the treadmills of our minds. The daily quiz, the weekly test, book reports, homework, exercises, show and tell, library work, term papers, the question, the answer. The answer, we knew, always existed. It was nice to find the best way there, but ultimately, it was the *right* answer that put you into the National Honor Society, that put you into college, that put you into . . .

It was significant that we were united at slumber parties, in speedball games, and in the lunchroom. Released from the necessity of labor, we could open our hearts to one another on the softball field and in the all-school assembly. A sea of youth sensed the unbroken, orgiastic surge of camaraderie, the equality of man, the possibilities for justice, and the potential of unified energy. We were humanized in a great mass of faces just like ours, and we were never to forget the ecstasy of togetherness.

The Cuban Crisis, the Berlin Wall, Nikita Khrushchev, Freedom 7, Barry Goldwater, Dag Hammarskjöld, and thalidomide all existed in an ordered universe. The easy security of the American home accommodated all and discovered that almost anything could happen and the new garage and the backyard grill still would stand. While the hamburgers cooked, however, the children starved. Glutted with the power to receive, we waited for the lesson on how to give until we could hold no more, and we vomited up our full minds and hearts.

The prophetic rumblings came from within that same home. We grew used to sights of dogs and fire hoses on a television screen that had once happily held both Spankie and Buckwheat. Medgar Evers, SNCC, the marches, James Meredith, and "We Shall Overcome" haunted our young laughter. We sensed the same beloved unity of our

football games that was at work in the sit-ins. "Segrega-
tion" and "integration" beat in our eardrums until one day
we had to leave the dinner tables in disgust, slamming the
bedroom doors on impossible arguments. I was taught
"God is love." I never really knew what was meant. I was
told, "Jesus died for your sins," and I could not recall any
misdeeds. My young world had been too stable, too ordered.

In 1967 with the cities rioting, I entered college. The
word was "psychedelic." LSD could be produced in any
high school chemistry lab, and the sound was amplified
until it penetrated the skin. The divorce rate and the war
were fattening themselves. Obituaries of area soldiers became more frequent than IBM promotions, but even as the
incongruities grew, our minds and our unique human
quality of reason fought for more answers to questions few
believed in. I began to fly frequently in Boeing jets,
reading for my next paper or the upcoming exam. I had
lived in four different states and as I flew, the distance between them shrank, the distance between countries shrank,
and the space between planets was reduced, but my
reading and thought led me down darker alleys which
were more and more removed from human activity. Somehow, one day I knew there was futility in the pursuit, for
the real questions were being asked on the streets. We had
been told that the rewards of a happy life were worthwhile
goals, but when we no longer believed that there was a
happy life, we were able to ask our own questions.

At the tender moment, we had seen the garish mask of
security revealed in its hideous complacency, its bland and
stupid nerves deadened to that which it shielded. By living
a good life we knew bad when we saw it. By moving unfet-
tered we knew chains. Because we understood only good

fortune we were acutely aware of injustice and since we believed that the material world could not restrict human potential, the realization dawned that we ourselves were our own worst enemies. Children of fortune, already starving, being hit by waves bigger than their boats, were now drowning.

We had watched our parents float off to calmer seas on fat rubber rafts that didn't seem to suit our bodies. Weighted down by our clothes, we discarded them. Naked, we were cold and dazed. The sea gorged on our flimsy crafts made of every Boy Scout knot we had ever tied, and we knew at last, metaphorically, we were on the street. We had to swim.

I am made much like you. When I discovered I could reason, I also discovered deep longings that went beyond reason. The computer age and I were born simultaneously, but in the end the mental tools I had so tediously developed could not tell me what stirred deep down inside when I gazed from the machines to the march of humanity on the television screen. I no longer wanted words, I wanted meanings. I no longer wanted to be told, I wanted to do. I no longer believed that there need be man-made divisions, for I knew there were commonalities and communities somewhere under the strife. I sensed that something had been overlooked. An error had been made that was costing us our campuses and our homes. My nation was smothering in its baby fat and I no longer believed in its goodness or in its way of life, but I did believe that the idea of man on which it was founded was sound because the validity of human essence was sound.

So, I set out to battle my mind, the instrument that had given me my experiences, my morals, and my security.

The time had come to reject my mind-oriented identity in a mind-oriented society. I no longer thirsted after the knowable but after the unknowable. In this sense, I was attempting to enlarge my concept of "knowledge" to include very ephemeral bits of information. Edmund Spenser was taken to heart when I read, "Why then should witlesse man so much misweene, That nothing is, but that which he hath seene?" A scorn for formalized education developed. How limited we had become in our zeal for truth! I saw my companions turning away also. We were becoming determined to bring the dichotomies together, to unite head and heart, thinking and feeling, and in so doing, heal the wounds and bridge the widening gaps.

Yes, I would call this a spiritual questing, for it is a seeking of that which is often only a sensing. A balance, an equilibrium, harmony, union, peace. It has many names but a single motive, which is to be in tune with one's whole self, one's fellows, and one's physical and metaphysical surrounds. America's Christianity had become secularized to the point where it no longer could serve as religion, as celebration of the fact of existence in total, and America's youth were demanding this celebration, with or without "religion." Perhaps we are simply spoiled children. We have had it all except the final desire—to know God. Yet I prefer to believe that it was a simple matter of wanting to regain the other half of our lives so that we would not be half-receiving, half-responding, half-human.

I began craving experience, from the simplest occurrences to chaotic events, yet my tools were ineffective. I was self-conscious, conditioned, and ignorant, then frustrated. To be sure, the hopelessness of the young in the spring of 1970 was a reflection of a spiritual as well as a political morass, for the unity we had achieved by meshing analysis, feeling, and action was savagely broken then in a million ways.

From nowhere, into my life and within this context of tension, came a personal loss so great that I found myself literally lifeless. The self with which I had lived for twenty-one years disappeared. It was not transformed or defeated, it simply vanished, leaving me mindless and, more important, without a soul. For months I touched without feeling, spoke without words, slept without rest, and thought without ideas. My vegetable state pervaded my biological as well as my psychological being and I arrived at the age-old abyss, believing there was no way to regain my humanness. But as I told you, one evening in December, I felt myself to be a part of something so much greater than anything I had ever known that from that time on, very slowly, my vision and my blood gained strength. My old belief that being human meant a larger totality than I had been led to believe was affirmed forever, and I knew that man was indeed a part of the harmonious cosmos, blending with and augmenting the shape of all existence.

I returned somewhat to formal religion, desiring expression in historic ritual because I felt linked not only with the present existence but with all ages past and future. Being familiar with Christianity, I turned most easily there; however, I consider myself less a Christian in many ways. Yet I, like so many of my contemporaries in their myriad ways, have become religious. I worship beauty and squalor, hatred and kindness. I celebrate poverty and wealth, disease and health. I praise the moment in which I am living, the sensations which I am receiving, the reactions I am returning, the space in which I am moving, and any other living organism present. I am faithful, for I am a believer and I have been rewarded by grace. In my open-

ness, every concretion or nuance of existence, be it a tor-
ment or a joy, affirms the magnificence of all creation.
Moving in unique liberation means responding more
wholly to situations and giving more completely of my
mind and abilities. From a state of utter self-loss, I have
gained a self more complete than I ever hoped for, one
with as much prowess as my intellect. Finally, my coexist-
ence with others has become highly sensitized. Vibrations
are plentiful because I know, even if the other person does
not, that he is human and therefore possesses the same
soul I have discovered. Often the person senses that I
know her or him already, even if it is a first acquaintance.
Preliminaries are forgotten and we quickly arrive at what
is meaningful in the meeting. My greatest hope now is that
I might always maintain this ability to be open.

## The Generation-Not-Buying-It

> . . . in those students, the suddenness, flare, joy,
> surprise, insight, uncharity, intolerance, the gnaw-
> ing and digging for the truth of things . . . those
> students, whose childhood had been war, whose
> youth is war, who have been handed a bill of
> goods in a chic package, and told, with the leer of
> the old con man, Go ahead, buy it. . . . And then,
> after repeated refusals to be hooked, the threat:
> Buy it, kid, or else.

The words are Dan Berrigan's, the priest-poet-felon, whose community with those who won't buy it has resulted in his ongoing exploration of the threat's *or else*.

He speaks of a generation "whose childhood had been war." In fact, for well over half those Americans now alive, the nuclear incineration of Hiroshima and Nagasaki was a prenatal event, a capsule of acid inherited in the recesses of conscience, not released until we realized (headlines of Strontium 90) that those weapons had been dissolved into our milk; that breasts were becoming radioactive; that our genes were the final test sites of atomic warheads.

"Whose childhood had been war, whose youth is war," observed Denise Levertov, in her poem, "Life at War." "We have breathed the grits of it in, all our lives . . ." In our childhood there was Korea, Guatemala, Montgomery, Cuba, Vietnam, Laos, Cambodia, Watts, the Dominican Republic, Selma, Harlem, Bedford Stuyvesant, more Vietnam.

In entertainment as in reality, our inheritance was war. There World War II had been institutionalized, the war

forever being reverenced, admired, its heroic deaths
marched in infinite procession, a daily lining up of Holly-
wood Germans and Japanese initiating us into body
counts and state worship. And in those movies, a studio-lit
image of ourselves—the vitamin-dominated, virtue-for-
tified nation-brand, a product enriching lucky bodies
twelve ways and easily superior to all the competition.

War was also, more subtly, our experience in schools.
There our lives were organized in thought periods spaced
with (so I remember them) firehouse bells. The daily
forced-march was into shiny-paged textbooks, a drill of
raised hands, tests, grades. School was our first and most
conclusive defeat by conscription, an involuntary servi-
tude so endowed with the state's incense, so mythologized,
that it was heresy to wonder, even silently, whether there
might be some seed of sanity in our early urges to escape
the agony of being buried alive between desk and chair.
For in effect school was (as Ivan Illich has noted) a gov-
ernment-inspected One, True Church, the fount of secular
orthodoxy complete with its liturgies of flag devotion and
celebrations of the Feasts of St. Custer, St. Washington, St.
Paul of Revere, and other Church Fathers of Manifest
Destiny. The school was even the source of pastoral guid-
ance—assurance continually renewed that daily reception
of the sacraments of consumer life would eventually assure
salvation in Florida or California.

In the state-adapted churches, an auxiliary role in the
continuing war was allotted, that anonymous, conscripted,
consumer life might be properly baptized so long as the
flag was kept in proximity to the altar. Sermons and parochial education assured God's affection for all that preserved the church's tax exemption.

The war continued as we were drafted into genitally organized vocations and identities. It continued in the gray air and the ammonia water that had become technology's insignia. It continued in cattle-car transportation systems. It continued in uniformed clothes and vocabularies. It continued in all the rehearsed responses of a way of death whose final logic was the burning of huts and of humans wherever the America-destined flow of wealth, or its missionary intentions, were challenged.

*"Go ahead, buy it."*

In fact, many more of us would have bought it had it not been, to name only several, for Rosa Parks, Jack Kerouac, Allen Ginsberg, Thomas Merton, and Dorothy Day.

It was Rosa Parks who, in Montgomery, Alabama, on December 1, 1955, finding herself "too tired" to resign her bus seat to a white man, stayed put until arrested—and that simple act of nonviolent resistance became the archetype of something that has so multiplied in America that perhaps hope has, at last, some historical justification for us.

It was she who turned less to courts than to life-style as the crucial means of change, who reminded us of the negative foundation of affirmative action: the revolutionary freedom not only to form No with our lips, but to live it out even when our purchase and obedience are demanded by presidents and generals. Rosa Parks was "too tired."

Kerouac and Ginsberg—and Gary Snyder and others—were those who became the contemporary equivalent of the long-forgotten Desert Fathers: those intense people who, in the fourth century, began fasting from all they were supposed to consume, from ideologies as well as meat, from ecclesiastical as well as government bureaucracy; a fast from having, from respectability, from all vestiges of a safety-deposit-box-protected future. Like the

Beats, they were Cain-fathered Adams and Eves, dollar-ig-
noring children of hard-core consumers; proof that, on miraculous occasion, figs do grow from thistles. They made
visible the amazing possibility that there is a way of escap-
ing the inheritance of murder, the possibility that we could
say, with life-style instead of wish: *The violence stops here.
The war stops here. The suppression of the truth stops here.*
As Dan Berrigan said at Catonsville.

Ginsberg's *Howl,* Kerouac's *On the Road*—and the
strange partnership of these with Thomas Merton's *Seven
Storey Mountain* and *Seeds of Contemplation*—all had in
common the same desert, the same life: a desert life, in
every detail; that is, thriving where life is officially declared to be impossible; or thriving with a style of life that
is advertised as being miserable—a life-style that stub-
bornly refuses to endorse the authorized myth that happiness comes when the self is thickly insulated from a birth-
right of vulnerability.

They took pleasure, as would any monk, man or
woman, with or without ecclesiastical credentials, in the
zen koan: "The thief left it behind!/. . . the moon at the
window."

It was Dorothy Day, founder of the Catholic Worker,
who took the monastic style and assertion (that happiness
has something to do with God, with acceptance of vulnerability, with love, with worship—even if called poetry
readings; and not much to do with guaranteed security)
and joined that with the need for some to remain close to
need, to resist the institutions of violence, to bring into
being—out of the experiments of one's communal life—an
alternative life-style that sheds no blood, that is peace-
making, that is at peace.

Dorothy Day began the Catholic Worker, and among

those influenced, at least indirectly, were all these persons mentioned already here (one of my earliest memories of the Catholic Worker is Ginsberg chanting his poem "Kaddish" on the sagging second floor in the Chrystie Street house).

The Catholic Worker people lived on a kind of desert too—sometimes in jail cells, the usual consequence of resistance; or the more routine desert of the Bowery, where those of no great interest to anyone were allowed to attempt survival; or their desert was the house of hospitality, in which a great many of the guests were sick in mind and body. It was desert because no one subscribing to the consumer dream could imagine we could be happy in such a life: "must be masochists." Yet most who came for something other than soup were there to be happy. And, remarkably often, we were. On tenement roofs at sunrise, in amateur, Anglicized Gregorian, some chanted the psalms and other ancient prayers with the fervor of readings in coffeehouses. At night, under pressed-tin ceilings in $25-a-month rooms, there were often beer and candlelight, cheese, records played on a cheap machine, long hours of talk. Even selling the paper on the streets—a penny a copy, as it remains—was a welcome event, and was how we got the change for cheese and beer.

I am speaking of a relatively few, of which I was one, who went directly the Catholic Worker route, and who were primarily influenced by Merton and Ginsberg and the others. Yet there have been very similar consequences for a great many persons; few of the mentors others might name in explaining their changes would not be of the same stamp; even persons but one step removed from the several I have named were catalysts for countless others who have, in turn, been as influential as their teachers were.

The ripples have produced their own waves, the news getting around—variously formulated—that "surely life is more than food, the body more than clothes." It has been analogous to the growth of the early Christian community; the current example chooses to say, as did St. Paul, "They call us dead people—but it is we who are alive."

AUSTIN WARREN:

## The Crisis of the Young

I find it ever harder to write or speak on an abstract or theoretical subject—those subjects being (if within my competence) literary or spiritual—without an autobiographical approach, without making my own identity clear by defining where I stand, what I have at stake, and how I came to believe as I do. The kind of vision at which such subjects aim cannot be had without initial commitment; and presumably the objectivity of which they are ultimately capable is a sum total and synthesis of competent and committed personal and private visions.

I am ethnically Anglo-Saxon Protestant (ethnically Protestant, not spiritually). Born in 1899, I was reared a Methodist. In my high school days, I was a Fundamentalist—indeed, what would now be called a "Jesus freak," though, unlike current varieties, I did not set up on my own: I remained within my sect and respected the clergy even though I thought my father's half-witted hired man holier than any of them. The gospel hymns were my treasury and delight.

While I was a Latin major at Wesleyan, I became a Swedenborgian, and a member of the Church of the New Jerusalem founded to promulgate the "heavenly doctrines" of Swedenborg. My period in this church introduced me to mysticism, allegory and symbolism, exegesis of Scripture, and comparative religion. It made a Christian Platonist out of me and a Christian Gnostic—that is, one who distinguishes the esoteric wisdom of the Church accessible to "knowers," spiritual intellectuals, from the superstitious and legalistic or magical practices associated

with popular Catholicism or the moralism of popular Protestantism.

In my twenties I became, by conviction and confirmation, a communicant of the Episcopal Church, the American version of the Anglican Church (that is, the now
worldwide Church of England); and my allegiance, however qualified, was to the Anglo-Catholic party in the Anglican Church, that party which holds the whole Anglican
Church to be, by historic succession of bishops and by its
creeds and sacraments, an integral part of the Catholic
Church, the other integral parts being the Roman Catholic
Church and the Eastern Orthodox (Greek and Russian).

In my forties I was influenced for a time by Kierkegaard; but I rejected his influence after a while as tending
to make me proud of my psychological complexion and as
putting the claims of religion in so exacting a fashion as to
make it impossible to be "saved." He was, I found, even
more rigorous than the William Law who wrote that *Serious Call to a Devout and Holy Life,* which had so impressed
Dr. Johnson before me. I turned back to the Christian Humanism, coupled with Quietist mysticism, of Fénelon, the
seventeenth-century Roman Catholic archbishop who, of
all single spiritual guides, has most quieted my soul, stead-
ied my course, and ministered to irenic wisdom.

Also in my forties I was much influenced by Aldous
Huxley's *Perennial Philosophy,* an anthology of passages
from the saints and mystics of all the "higher religions"—
including Eckhart, St. Bernard, St. Francis of Sales, Fénelon, and Law as well as Hindus, Buddhists, and Sufis—
together with an illuminating commentary by the anthol-
ogizer. It is Huxley's contention (and I think he demonstrates it) that within all the "higher religions" there is contained a yet "higher," an esoteric, religion. For some rea-

sons (partly, I should think, "personal"), Huxley, on the basis of this, became a Vedantist (an esoteric follower of the Hindu religion), while I (like Dom Aelred Graham, in his *Zen Catholicism*) have concluded that, as the highest spirituality is found also, even if not always on the surface, in the Catholic Christian tradition, there is no good reason for a Westerner reared in the Christian tradition to reject his own heritage for that of an alien culture.

The spiritual experiences of my fifties were three: I had five or six years of close association with the Eastern Orthodox Church in its Greek form: without leaving the Episcopal Church—indeed, with the permission of my Anglican confessor, I did my regular Sunday duty at the Greek church. I studied the liturgy, continued and developed my interest in Orthodox iconology, and much profited from reading such nineteenth- and twentieth-century Russian spiritual writers as Soloviev, Berdyaev, Bulgakoff, and Lossky. Then I suffered (and was enriched by) a severe psychic breakdown—a relief and release and emancipation. And, lastly, I had a number of periods of close association with a community of Anglican Benedictine monks and their Prior, a man of tenderness and holy wisdom.

In these last decades I have also managed what, for a convert to Anglicanism or Roman Catholicism, is difficult: an ecumenism which includes a sympathetic recognition of the genuine spiritual values of orthodox Protestantism —especially in my own ancestral Methodism and in the ancestral religion of New England, the Calvinist tradition of Cotton Mather and, most of all, of Jonathan Edwards and his disciples, the Protestant Scholastics, as I have called them. Wesley, the preacher of "heart religion" and holiness, and Edwards, the philosophical theologian, have taken their place with Origen, Andrewes, Fénelon, and von Hügel among my "saints." [1]

From 1920 to 1968 I was a university teacher of English, or (as I preferred to say) of literature, or (shall I say) of "culture" or the humanities, of whatever I knew and hoped, by verbal discourse or dialogue or sheer osmosis, I could impart to the young. For most of my life, I practiced in three forms: I gave public lectures, taught seminars and other small groups (esoteric instruction), and privately educated those who sought me out as one who could, as the Friends say, "speak to their condition." And I wrote books, not as means of professional advancement, or even, primarily, as a part of my professional obligation (though I do indeed old-fashionedly consider "research" or close critical study eventuating in writing and publication as well-nigh obligatory parts of the academic's life). I wrote: subjectively, because I found it for me an indispensable instrument of self-definition and intellectual clarification, a method of therapy and of salvation, and objectively, on the relation of religion (Roman Catholic, Anglican, and Protestant) to the arts (specifically poetry) and to culture.

Both in religion and in education I managed to stay within their respective established and institutional forms, the university and the church. I say "managed to"; for I am at ease only on the periphery of both. I have not been able to function well as a committee member, a party worker, a vestryman; and I do not wish to be an administrator (*Nolo episcopari*). But I am not so ungrateful as to hold administrators in contempt. To them I owe, at minimum, gratitude for providing a framework within which public libraries can be collected, classrooms and sanctuaries can be built, and I and others like me can lead a relatively contemplative life, sharing their time between their own prayers and studies and the direction of the studies of the young or the maintenance of the public worship of God.

I have outlined my own spiritual chronicle as a preliminary to my reflections on the current situation in university and church, the religious situation of today, and the spiritual plight of the young.

I belong, like Tillich, with those men whose lot it is to live "on the boundary," with those who are "torn between." I have myself stayed within church, university, and (I may add) state partly out of skepticism (the evils of institutions are inherent in the nature of institutions, and are not to be abolished by substituting a new set of institutions: institutions are, for mankind, a necessary evil) and partly out of steady faith in the importance of continuity. These reasons probably mark me by intellectual constitution as a conservative, even though a liberal conservative.

But, throughout my adult life, I have understood and sympathized with the young, have either taken their side or attempted to mediate between it and the administration, the powerful elders. I still instinctively feel for the critical and rebellious young; but the present situation is difficult for me to face. The tension between the establishments and their young critics is more extreme than any I have known. I try hard to sympathize with the young; but they seem to me so unlovely, so intolerant, so opinionated, so ungenerous. I dislike their conformist dress, which caricatures that of the really poor. I dislike their limited vocabulary, their designed or feigned inarticulateness. I dislike their economic dependence on the very parents whom they despise. I find them inimical to any culture save their own limited and provincial sub- and counter-culture, and arrogant in their ignorance of history.

Undoubtedly what irritates me most in the current young is their sense of uniqueness and their pride in it. I was, in my time, a strange, an odd young man, who fitted ill with my college contemporaries preparing for careers in business, who was disdainful of the American ethnically Protestant middle class in which I was reared, and disdainful of the American identification of progress with technology, of civilization with modern comforts and big business. But it was a joy to me to discover, in the classes of Irving Babbitt at Harvard, that I was an oddity only to provincial eyes, that in my classical humanism (with its Eastern equivalent in the humanism of Confucius) and my Catholic-orientated religion (with its Eastern equivalent in Buddhism), I was heir to great, to perennial, traditions.

And so that remarkable man Emerson (though mostly on the side of the Future, not of History) had pleasure in pointing out, to the conservatives of his time, that the Transcendentalism of New England in the 1840s was substantially identical with the "way of thinking [which], falling on Roman days, made Stoic philosophers . . . , on superstitious times, made prophets and apostles; on popish times, made protestants and monks . . . ; on prelatical times, made Puritans and Quakers. . . ."

If (as it is a commonplace to remark) our period has its frightening analogies to the breakdown of the Roman empire, with its welfare program of bread and circuses, its threatenment from without, its corruption and decadence within, its influx of Eastern religions and its disputations between rival brands of existential philosophy, it belongs more immediately, especially as it concerns our intellectuals and our young, to the sequence which began with the

Industrial movement and *its* counterstatement in the form of the Romantic movement, German, French, English, and American. And most immediately it reminds one of the American 1830s and 1840s—the period of Transcendentalism and the Reform movement. It reminds us of Transcendentalism with its self-reliance (the "self" ambiguous between the idiosyncratic self and the Hindu True Self or Atman), its appeal to the "higher laws," its turning to the Sacred Books of the East; and it reminds us of the many-sided Abolitionist movement, into which went the most spiritually intense energy of the period's activists, and of the Utopian Socialism exemplified in Brook Farm and the Perfectionism of Oneida.

Four lectures that Emerson gave at Boston in 1841 and 1842—"Man the Reformer," "Lecture on the Times," "The Conservative," and "The Transcendentalist"—all speak with remarkable aptness (or "relevance") to our own times. (He makes a better, a more philosophic, case for conservatism than most conservatives could make.)

Emerson speaks, with especial insight and tenderness, of his younger contemporaries (such, presumably, as Charles Newcomb, a picturesque member of Brook Farm), those who most closely resemble the "loafers" and "inviters of their souls" among our hippies. There were, then, too, those who, in Paul Goodman's phrase, "grew up absurd," finding no proper work—those who, rather than accept work they could not find worth doing, did none—who (as Emerson says in "The Transcendentalist") "feel the disproportion between their faculties and the work offered them; they prefer to ramble in the country and perish of ennui to the degradation of such charities and such ambitions as the city can propose to them." They are lonely; yet they will make no concessions to adult and conformist

society; they are "the most exacting and extortionate critics. They prolong their childhood in this wise: of doing
nothing, but making immense demands on all the gladia-
tors in the lists of action and fame." They have looked at
the pursuits of their elders and found none to satisfy:
"from the liberal professions to the coarsest manual labor,
and from the courtesies of the academy and the college to
the conventions of the cotillon room and the morning call,
there is [they find] a spirit of cowardly compromise and
seeming which implies a frightful scepticism, a life without
love, and an activity without aim." So they idle; so they
wait, critical, expectant.

What became of Emerson's young and not-so-young
friends as they grew older? As Emerson himself asks, what
has become of the young idealists of yesteryear? The utopian communities, all save those which (like that of the
Shakers) were founded upon a definitely religious basis,
came to an end in a relatively short time, as the communes
of today will presumably do. But I am aware of no former
members of Brook Farm, the most articulate, best-docu-
mented of the communities, who were not, after they returned to that outside world which they called "civilization," proud of having once had, in their youth, the
idealism to engage in so utopian, so model-making, a ven-
ture. Some few drifted off into vacuity and day-dreaming;
but most of them managed some honorable substitute
fulfillment of their aspirations: they became Roman Catholics (Father Hecker, the founder of the Paulists, was a
Brook Farmer); they became musicians or artists or writers or editors; most of the women made appropriate marriages: Margaret Fuller, their feminist ally though never
literal member, became a journalist, a feminist, a valiant

worker for the Italian Revolutionary Mazzini, and finally a mother and a martyr.

The situation of the young in our time, of the spiritual questers among them at least, is not totally unique. Certainly there is a difference between the *now* crisis and other crises—most clearly, a quantitative one. The disaffected young—chiefly university students or university dropouts or their allies—are far more numerous than ever before. There are far more wandering hippies than, in the Middle Ages, there were Wandering Scholars; and their travels take them to more remote places; they are, at least so far as capitalist countries go, international. Whenever the Industrial Revolution has had time enough to succeed, it has brought such material advantages to the middle class that many of the sons of that class find its good things not finally good, only "status symbols." While the poor of the industrialized capitalist countries and the poor of the Third World are in need of the necessities of life, while the Blacks, having the necessities, want automobiles and color TV—those who have "had all these things from their youth up," the relatively rich young rulers, find they still lack something, something to give significance to their lives.

To these ultimate questions about ultimate values there are, so far as I know, no new answers. We know of the "relatively rich" for whom it is so difficult to choose objects for Christmas exchange, who "have everything." We can envisage as possible some remote time when all the people of all the world will "have everything" and many will still be unsatisfied.

The finer spirits in any age will have to betake themselves to values which are neither material goods, nor status symbols, nor means to ends; they will have to aim at activities, or states of being, which are ends in themselves. They will have to aim at a self-fulfillment which is (differentially viewed) a self-forgetfulness, a life-saving which is a life-losing. These values, which are ends in themselves, remain: the love of art (esthetic contemplation), the love of knowledge (science), the love of wisdom (philosophy), the love of man (philanthropy), and the love of God (religion).

Sooner or later the disaffected young idealists will have to rejoin society, rejoin the human race. If they have reason to reject the standards, faulty indeed, of their parents, the middle-class America in which they grew up, let them remember that they have grandparents and great-grand-parents and ancestors. They are "encompassed about by a cloud of witnesses" and a "choir Invisible" of martyrs, saints, and sages, even in the spiritual history of America. Every family of minds has its own heroic progenitors.

1. For irenic views of the spiritual values in Protestantism written by converts, cf. Ronald Knox, *Enthusiasm* (1950), especially for its tribute to John Wesley, and Louis Bouyer, *Orthodox Spirituality and Protestant and Anglican Spirituality* (1969).

THOMAS PHELAN:

## Men Have Always Climbed Mountains

The present spiritual quest of young people is by no means a completely new phenomenon. One can safely say, from the recorded experience of the race, that it is as old as the human spirit. Primitive rites of passage as well as the Judeo-Christian Passover models suggest that life is a pilgrimage, even a pursuit. The theme of the return runs through all of human history. It was Augustine in the early fifth century of our era who remarked that God has made us for himself and our hearts can find no rest except in him. The American experience has been first a hoped-for rediscovery of paradise and now a realization and disillusionment that it is not.

Often when a society is plagued by social and economic insecurity, the spiritual quest emerges as a major theme of the time. This is in no way a put-down of the present spiritual quest. Rather, it is to say that to help us understand the contemporary phenomenon we must look back.

Millenarian sects or movements have been always with us. Norman Cohn in his classic work, *The Pursuit of the Millennium*, lists in his introduction the elements of millenarian salvation as:

(a) collective, in the sense that it is to be enjoyed by the faithful as a collectivity;

(b) terrestrial, in the sense that it is to be realized on this earth and not in some other-worldly heaven;

(c) imminent, in the sense that it is to come both soon and suddenly;

(d) total, in the sense that it is utterly to transform life on earth, so that the new dispensation will be no mere improvement on the present but perfection itself;

(e) miraculous, in the sense that it is to be accomplished by, or with the help of, supernatural agencies.

There are innumerable examples of millenarianism throughout the Christian age. Let me mention one which will sound as though it could be happening today in Vermont or western Massachusetts or Berkeley—or in one or the other of your friendly local communes. The phenomenon was called the heresy of the Free Spirit. The followers were gnostics intent upon their own individual salvation; but the gnosis at which they arrived was a quasi-mystical anarchism—an affirmation of freedom so reckless and unqualified that it amounted to a total denial of every kind of restraint and limitation.

The initiates of the Free Spirit were after the mystical experience. But they were intensely subjective, acknowledging no authority at all save their own experiences. In their eyes the church was at best an obstacle to salvation, at worst a tyrannical enemy—in any case an outworn institution which must now be replaced by their own community, seen as a vessel for the Holy Spirit. The adept's belief was that he had attained a perfection so absolute that he was incapable of sin. It was permissible for him, even incumbent on him, to do whatever was commonly regarded as forbidden. What emerges, among other things, is an eroticism which, far from springing from a carefree sensuality, possessed above all a symbolic value as a sign of spiritual emancipation. The heresy of the Free Spirit flourished, incidentally, from around A.D. 1200 until about 1320.

More important, however, than looking backward at other historical movements is that we should attempt to see where the present experience stands in relation to the Christian tradition. By tradition I mean much more than knowledge, tale, belief or custom transmitted from one generation to another. I mean that we live in a continuum. We have come from somewhere, and are presently at some place, and will move further along in due time. The past and the future are indispensable parentheses around the present, and the total is a living whole. Tradition is not a dead past, but a living historical line in which we now stand.

This being the case, it is important for us, as Western Christians essentially, to understand our Western Christian tradition of spirituality. But first let me say a word about spirituality, or spiritual life.

Man enjoys what we usually call an interior life. This interior life is basically our self-consciousness developing as intellection and freedom. When our interior life develops not in isolation, but in the awareness of a spiritual reality that is beyond individual consciousness, specifically a transcendent reality, then interior life is more properly called spiritual life. If we cared to go one step further, we would say that if the spirit known in the spiritual life is recognized not only as something, but as someone, then the spiritual life is a religious life as well. I suppose we might add that interior life tends to develop into spiritual life which, in turn, orients itself no less spontaneously toward some form of religious life.

The Christian spiritual life is dynamic; it is always moving toward the full development of a life which must be wholly human and at the same time wholly personal. The Christian grows in this way in a relationship with God, who is not only himself a person, but the personal being par excellence. Further, Christian spirituality assumes that God, in Christ, has made himself known to us by his own words and his own acts as someone.

In Christianity the spiritual life starts from faith, which is the openness and the assent we give to the word of God. No one really becomes himself, a person, except in dialogue. For the Christian, God has spoken and continues to speak by and in the Church. In faith Christian man responds to God's word spoken in time. In this way we are given not simply life in general, but God's own life and the possibility, and in fact the capacity, to love even as he loves. This is really what Christians believe.

In the last paragraph I introduced the word "Church" when I said that God continues to speak to us by and in the Church. "Church" is more often than not an unacceptable word, especially among young people. But those who find it unacceptable are hung up on the institution, which they see as all too human to be a vehicle for God's work in the world. They see the Church only as a particular institution with all its shortcomings hanging out all over. Let me say, however, that I use "Church" in a more biblical way as the assembly of people, Christians, which has been and is being spoken to by God, and which recognizes the word as God's word and feels compelled to respond. This assembly is drawn together by a common hearing of the word and a common need to respond in a more or less common way. The Church is therefore a community. As such, and in the present order, it is an institution; but institution apart from community is no Church at all.

Having digressed to establish the way in which I use the word "Church," let me now pick up on the description of Christian spiritual life as it is revealed to us in our tradition. As I have said, Christian spiritual life starts with the word of God and the ability to listen to that word, which we call faith. The word is the revelation of a person to a person, an I to a you. Man, the you, receives the word in the faith community where it is still animated by the presence of the person who spoke it, where the Spirit who inspired it is still active.

This is what we experience in a very particular way in the celebration of the liturgy. In fact, the definition of Church which I have just given is also description of the liturgical celebration. In the liturgical celebration par excellence, the Eucharist, the faithful are assembled, and the word is proclaimed and received as a transforming reality, and the assembly so transformed feels compelled to make a response by offering the sacrifice of Christ represented under the symbols of bread and wine. God, not to be outdone, offers in return the banquet, the bread from heaven which gives life to the world. You can't separate liturgy from Church or Church from liturgy. In our tradition the two are irrevocably bound together.

In the context I have now established, which is the process of spiritual life in our tradition, there are three important elements: prayer, sacrament, asceticism. Let me introduce each one briefly. They are all part of our tradition. I think we find them in one way or another in the spiritual quest of any age. They are certainly present in all the best contemporary individual and group spiritual endeavors.

If word proclaimed and faith response are the basic elements in Christian spirituality, then we are already talking about dialogue, the dialogue which is prayer. God speaks; we respond. We listen, we speak. Much could be said about prayer as dialogue and about its forms: individual and communal, vocal and mental, meditative and contemplative, passive and active. Suffice it to say that prayer is very close to the most basic elements of Christian spirituality, and one of the three essential components of our spiritual tradition. Prayer is conversation between the lover and the beloved. The Christian must be both reflective and actively engaged in conversation with God, which is possible only in the dimension to which we have been introduced by faith. The Christian lives the same life as everyone else, but he lives it in the faith dimension. Christian prayer is carried on in the faith dimension.

Another component of our spiritual tradition is sacrament. Faith is the opening of the soul, largely achieved in the prayer context, to the word of God coming to us in and by the Church. The word of God is concentrated in the Christian core fact, the mystery which is none other than Christ himself and his cross experience. But, in the Church, this mystery is not merely proclaimed. Rather, with the very authority of God, it is proclaimed as present. It is represented, rendered present for us and in us, by sacrament or sacred symbol. Sacrament is the mystery really present in symbol to the man of faith for his participation in it and the resulting spiritual growth. Christ's experience touches man and becomes his experience.

Beyond sacramental life there is the third element, Christian asceticism, which is the daily effort to make life accord with faith. Asceticism implies no condemnation of the world or our body, but a realization that we are fallen from integrity and that our own efforts of fasting, austerity, abstention, and mortification, done in faith, are necessary for our reintegration. This is the human condition. Man is essentially good, but wounded and in need of healing. This is the only context in which the Beatitudes, for example, can be properly understood. They are faith-life ways, ways that make sense only in the context of faith, that offer us healing, reintegration.

Christian asceticism is an asceticism of death and resurrection, an asceticism of the cross. Baptism is our first experience of this. As Paul tells us, we have died with Christ in baptism and are now risen to a new kind of life. Life in the world provides daily opportunities. Our work, our married life, our motherhood and fatherhood, our almsgiving, our prayer, our fasting and moderation in self-discipline—all provide opportunities for asceticism in the faith dimension. In this way we are purified of our vices and return from the disobedience of sin to the obedience to the Father, which is best modeled in Jesus' own life. Thus our life becomes a series of conversions, and the basic Christian imperative of change (metanoia) is realized. We change, and our change is growth toward self-realization, fulfillment, salvation.

Through asceticism and prayer, and the religious experience which is offered through sacramental life, man is brought to the illumination which is a goal of the Christian life, and to the union which is the stuff of self-fulfillment.

I have reviewed quite briefly our Christian tradition of the spiritual life so that we might bring into critical focus the present spiritual quest of the young. There is an element of difference which immediately comes to mind. Primitive man celebrated nature as medieval man celebrated God. Cave paintings and cathedrals are evidences of this. Modern man became aware of himself, attentive to his own state of mind, in such a way that modern spiritual life was not able to abstract from it. In my own Roman Catholic tradition both Carmelite and Jesuit schools of spirituality in their time took this fact into account. I believe that there is a new, postmodern fact to be taken into account today and for the future. We have begun to develop a social consciousness beyond self-consciousness. The new consciousness *is* a social consciousness.

Reich's "Consciousness Three" says it well, but unfortunately without taking into account human nature's fall and its need for salvation. The new social consciousness is not the same as yesterday's social consciousness. It goes beyond brotherly love and service to the community and patriotism toward the nation. It is first a world-awareness, facilitated by the speed of the media. More, it is a consciousness that what affects men in Bombay or Vladivostok or Canton or Cape Town does really affect us in Worcester or Boise or Natchez or even Gary. Further, it is a consciousness that the good things of the good life ought to be shared by all, even if this means that the haves have less while the have-nots have a little more. It is also a conviction that all, even the inexperienced, have something to share, and that all should participate in the decision-making processes by which their lives and their futures are determined. If before there were the manipulators and the manipulated, that is no longer acceptable; manipulated man will no longer have it.

The new consciousness often takes an indifferent attitude toward the old work ethic. It is inclined to turn against the material rewards and the competitiveness that have motivated so much American progress. It can do so because it has enjoyed a generation of economic security. When the mood appears apocalyptic, when chaos seems about to swallow up the world we know, it turns to reading and meditation and carpentry to "get its head together." And, thus established, it is ready to celebrate the unexpected and the new. It looks for alternate vocations, not taking its educational equipment overseriously. It revives the old mutual-aid societies by creating such new free-wheeling institutions as free stores and free schools as alternatives to having to cope with the business world and the academy. It does not believe that more is better but that better is more.

This new social consciousness is having and will have profound effects upon Christian spiritual life. For example we need to rediscover the Church in the way in which I have spoken of it as the assembly of the faithful. Community and the experience of it is an important thing. Prayer frequently needs a communal context. Our asceticism must take into account the disadvantaged. Can we live aloof in the suburbs while so many live in misery in the decaying inner cities? Can we use the Vietnamese to shore up our national and industrial postures? Can we allow ourselves to continue to be co-opted by establishments or must we now emerge as the critic of all establishments?

Social consciousness is an integral element of the spiritual quest of the young. It is the healthy aspect of the present spiritual revival. We might even go so far as to speak of the new social consciousness as a moral revolution. However, at the same time there are signs of a possible retreat from reality which is camouflaged as the search for profound experience. So many are "getting it all together" that "the movement" has pretty well collapsed. The trip is inward via Zen and yoga and witchcraft and mysticism—even the Pentecostal thing. Not that any of these things are necessarily inimical to social awareness and involvement. But, de facto, 1971 was the year when America cooled off—and moved inward away from social realities. Some of our young have been Agnewized. Some are disillusioned and feel guilty because of the collapse of spring 1970's momentary Camelot. Many, many are just plain apathetic—about everything except perhaps their own college grades. The threat of no work for many of the best educated of the land raises the specter of economic insecurity.

The danger of the postmodern age is the danger of the modern age, narcissism. When you turn inward you may get lost in yourself, more out of touch with reality and, therefore, more out of touch with the God, who is the only guarantee of our ultimate fulfillment. Enstacy or narcissism may occasion the same withdrawal symptoms as often characterize ecstasy.

There is another present danger which is not new but has been with us for all the centuries of Christ's coming. It is the danger of millenarianism, the danger which has its origins in the book of Revelation, where it is suggested that after his second coming Christ would establish a messianic kingdom on earth and would reign over it for a thousand years before the last judgment. We have already indicated the nature of the danger inherent in millenarian movements when we discussed the heresy of the Free Spirit.

In conclusion, I would make this observation: The spiritual quest is in general happening outside the Church. It reflects a disillusionment with the Church. This, to my mind, is dangerous not so much for the Church as for the quest itself. The quest needs the Church to keep it straight. To be able to perform this function, the Church needs to rediscover itself. Only then can it act as critic and guide to those who make the spiritual quest. Campus ministry, because it deals with the young people caught up in the spiritual quest, must *be* the Church—the real Church that I have attempted to define and describe. It must as Church know and provide what is good and healthy by way of spiritual life. It must as Church act as critic of what spiritual stuff is happening. This to me means acquaintance with the tradition, alertness to the changes of the times, perhaps prophetic leadership, sympathetic direction, etc. Only by such strong stands can we save many from further disillusionment and move the spiritual quest back into the bosom of a reborn Church in which it can really flourish.

CAROLINE AND JAMES SCHRAG:

## Seeking Truth

Working with a wide range of young people over the past several years has led us to encounter many forms of search for meaning in life, some bizarre, some courageous, and some shallow. As young Quakers working frequently with high school and college-aged young people of many denominations, we have found many of these young people to be looking for an honest and meaningful life. They are also very concerned about *how* to go about changing the world, and *whether* change is possible.

There is, of course, no single cause of youth's spiritual search; a phenomenon as complicated as this has many causes. We will discuss here what we see as some of the major causes of this search. Although we separate these causes for purposes of analysis, any given individual is likely to combine several or all of these reasons in her or his spiritual search. However, the amount of emphasis put on the various reasons by the person is extremely important. People pursuing a particular course of spiritual search mostly because their group is doing it and only slightly because they want more meaning in their lives are likely to remain unsatisfied, and probably need some assistance. On the other hand, a person who feels spiritually called to pursue some course of search, who is doing it simply because it is what's right, will probably be much more sure of herself or himself, and less vulnerable to petty group pressures.

The first reason that we see for this search is an attempt by young people genuinely to pursue truth. It involves a sense that an ultimately valid understanding of things can be reached from which one can cope with the present: a

basis for thinking, feeling, and *acting*. This often includes a conviction that there are awesome and mysterious dimensions to human life in the universe to which we should be open, despite the tendency of rationalistic Western civilization to minimize the importance of such experiences. Such searches may also take the form of discipleship, in which a person feels, quite simply, spiritually called to live the beliefs which she or he grows to feel are the truths by which the universe is governed. This often flows naturally to a deep commitment to making the world more just by living the kingdom of God here and now. As Martin Luther King once said, "I must be disobedient to *a* king in order that I can be obedient to *the* King."

A second reason for spiritual searching is the willing recognition by many young people that all of us need, to some extent, loving acceptance in some form of community. This sense of emotional security, of belonging, of sharing the most significant things in one's life with a community is of great significance in the spiritual searching of many young people. The impersonality of city life, of schools, and of many families often makes this a terribly pressing need. Sociologists and social psychologists admit that modern civilization hasn't really produced an effective way for people to meet this need.

A third reason for spiritual searching, true, we think, of an unfortunately large number of young people, is a rampant retreat from an impossible world, where those who want to make things better are scorned, hated, gassed, clubbed, jailed, and killed, while those who carry on the current murderous social patterns of our society are rewarded and idolized. A capsule summary of what many young people have told us (or others) might be as follows: "I drove all the way down to Washington, D.C., and spent forty-eight hours crammed in a hot, dirty jail cell, and Nixon still didn't end the war. I quit!" Having concluded from experience or observation that the world cannot be changed, people must look for meaning in other quarters. Whether it be drugs, Christianity, or Eastern religion, it's bound to be safer than trying to change the world, and hopefully more satisfying. This is not to say that drugs, Christianity, and Eastern religion aren't legitimate vehicles for spiritual searching in their own right; we feel that they certainly can be. But the motivation of a person coming to them because some other pursuit of meaning seems futile or too risky may well prevent that person from finding any real meaning in his or her new search.

Fourth, many people, young and old, simply follow the lead of whatever group of people is important in their life. Unless one is a leader, challenging the direction of a group in which one has some security and acceptance can be very threatening. Rather than face a possible unsettling of their whole way of life if they were to speak up and disagree, many people prefer to conform quietly to the dictates of their group.

Finally, some spiritual searches are pursued because many young people want very much to experience life firsthand. Growing up in their families and schools, they sense that they're being asked to accept a very sterilized version of what life is about. These young people see hypocrisy in, and feel far removed from, meaning in the life they've been brought up to live. Their response to this sometimes is an all-out pursuit of novelty, kicks, thrills, and new experiences. It may also be one reason for the strong attraction to self-sustaining communes, where people are doing the things they need to live, such as baking bread, growing large gardens, and fixing bicycles, cars, and houses themselves. There is meaning in doing these things directly rather than doing a job for money which then is spent for various goods and services that may or may not be necessary.

Returning to the fact that these motivations are very much combined and interwoven in actual people, what can be said about the overall nature of this spiritual search?

In many cases, young (and older) people come to this search with needs for love, community, and support which fire them with a lonely desperation. Others, injured by bitter experiences (alcoholic parents, brutal policemen, rape, disastrous marriages), bring to it a generalized anger and cynicism about life. Such motivations can lead to spiritual quests which are weak, perverted, or dangerous. In at least a few of the many groups making up the American peace movement, and at several recent college conferences on such topics as sexual roles, political styles, religions, and life-styles, we have seen diverse examples of searches which permitted or actually encouraged interpersonal hatred, rigid authoritarianism, blind obedience to leaders, and emotional confrontations based on destructive rather than constructive impulses. A sample rationale from some of these searches might be: "I'll get below the superficial level of communication and get to your 'emotional core' if I have to rip you open (emotionally or sexually) to do it." The kind of searches which *sometimes* permit such things to happen include encounter groups, sensitivity training, exclusive reliance on drugs, Jesus freaks, authoritarian communes and political groups, and, potentially, almost any religious group.

At least a few of the groups making up the American peace movement exhibit authoritarian rigidity in that members are pressured to accept decisions about group courses of action made by leaders without raising questions in their own minds, even though the leaders' decisions might affect them profoundly. "Jesus-freak" religious groups, Baba lovers, and some groups of Buddhist chanters, according to various accounts we have read or heard, fall victim to the same tendencies in that the elders or leaders of the various group units have the indisputable final word on the correct interpretation of the Bible or other holy source, and it doesn't sound as though they encourage much open discussion on such matters. Finally, at least a few radical therapy groups subscribe to a concept of "liberation" or "fulfillment," which seems ultimately to reduce all questions and relationships to negative emotions, to exclude open discussion, and to provide a stage for group manipulation by the leaders.

In summary, the intensity of people's needs—their very legitimate needs—may lead them to accept the frequently totalitarian demands of experimental religious or political groups, simply because they so badly need the acceptance of a group. Some fulfillment of this need is traded for unquestioning obedience to gurus, elders, and group pressure on questions of morality, religion, and appropriate social action (or lack of it).

RICHARD A. UNDERWOOD:

## Nietzsche's Child as Father of the "Sacred Yes"

In the first part of *Thus Spoke Zarathustra*, Zarathustra speaks on the "three metamorphoses of the spirit": "how the spirit becomes a camel; and the camel, a lion; and the lion, finally, a child." [1] The three stages of metamorphosis constitute a call, a new vocation, for man to become "human, all-too-human." The new calling emerges as the self-imposed task of man in response to Zarathustra's announcement, in the Prologue, of the "death of God." Given the premise, that is, of the death of God understood as the cultural fact of loss of faith in a supernatural God as the support system for the traditional values, man's task now is to create his own world of meaning and value. The consummation of this can be traced through the tasks of the three metamorphoses, represented by the camel, the lion, and the child.

The function of the camel, a beast of burden, is to kneel down "wanting to be well-loaded." But the task of the camel is to become a lion.

The lion, whose spirit says, "I will," must fight the great dragon whose name is "Thou Shalt." The great dragon is covered with scales, "and on every scale shines a golden 'thou shalt.'" The dragon says, "All value of all things shines on me. All value has long been created, and I am all created value. Verily there shall be no more 'I will.'" [2]

The first task of the lion, then, is to slay the great dragon, cast off the burden of "Thou shalt." In doing this the lion is establishing conditions in which "I will" might triumph. This is a "no-saying"; but because it is a no-saying to a no, the lion's act becomes a Sacred No. The Sacred No accomplishes not the creation of new values but, rather, "the creation of freedom for oneself for new creation." What the lion *cannot* do is create new values. For this a child is needed—and thus the second task of the lion is to become a child. Zarathustra asks, "But say, my brothers, what can the child do that even the lion could not do? Why must the preying lion still become a child?" And then the response: "The child is innocence and forgetting, a new beginning, a game, a self-propelled wheel, a first movement, a sacred 'Yes.' For the game of creation, my brothers, a sacred 'Yes' is needed: the spirit now wills his own will, and he who had been lost to the world now conquers his own world." [3]

Nietzsche's description of the dynamics of the three metamorphoses provides an appropriate context for interpreting positively the quest of the young. There is a sense in which the young represent the stage of the lion insofar as the struggle of the young is that of slaying the "great dragon." They are engaged not in *simple* destruction but in *dialectical* struggle: the negation of a negative. If we do not begin, in our interpretation, with the view that the quest of the young is an attempt at "the creation of freedom for new creation," then the elders are condemned simply to opposition.

Can the struggle of the young, manifested in their spiritual quest, be seen as metamorphosis into a "Sacred Yes"? Response to this depends upon at least two factors: (1) the perspective from which the established elders view the quest; (2) the effectiveness of the struggle being carried out by the young. In the end, however, it is the young themselves, not the elders, who represent the "great dragon," who must answer this second question.

Where, then, are the young to discover the resources for metamorphosis into health and wholeness in the wake of the values that have fled? The time of the young seems to be one of a "double not": the no-more of the "Thou shalt" and the not-quite-yet of the "I will." Both generations, theirs and ours, seem to have reached a moment of profound turning: the source is being sought in a different direction and the direction has to do with the rediscovery of inwardness. What this means can be seen in the poem by Delmore Schwartz, another master of the preceding generation.

> I waken to a calling,
> A calling from somewhere down, from a great height,
> Calling out of pleasure and happiness,
> And out of darkness, like a new light,
> A delicate ascending voice,
> Which seems forever rising, never falling
> Telling all of us to rejoice,
> To delight in the darkness and the light,
> Commanding all consciousness forever to rejoice! [4]

This poem seems to characterize in positive fashion the essential task in the quest of the young: the task, that is, of recovering the authenticity of what Paul Tillich referred to as "the depth dimension." The tragedy is that the established orders of the past, far from facilitating this task of recovery, seem actually to impede it. The young have been thrust out on their own, required to explore the terra incognita of their own deep destiny with guides and maps that seem terribly lacking. But then this, of course, is the challenge awaiting the metamorphosis of lion into child.

1. *Thus Spoke Zarathustra* in *The Portable Nietzsche*, ed. Walter Kaufmann (New York: The Viking Press, 1954, 1962), p. 137.

2. *Ibid.,* p. 139.

3. *Ibid.*

4. Delmore Schwartz, *Summer Knowledge: New and Selected Poems, 1938–58* (Garden City: Doubleday & Co., 1959), p. 211.

# II

## The Quest for Direction

My new boots skidded on boulders slick with
frost.
I scrambled up scree inch by inch, numb hand
above hand,
Raising my eyes to the sky beyond the rock.

DANIEL BURKE:

## The Sources of Ambiguity

Despite the fact of a decade of work on or around a university campus, I often find myself driven to the conclusion that I know very little about the spiritual quest of the young. Perhaps it is because in matters of the spirit I am influenced by the Zen maxim: "He who knows, does not say; he who says, does not know." Perhaps it is my difficulty with the conceit involved in commenting on someone else's experience. Or perhaps it is a reluctance to contribute anything that could possibly add to the unhealthy mind-set of "them" and "us" that already exists between generations. Are "their" crises really so different from "ours"? I have heard an affirmative answer to that question from both sides of the "gap," but I remain unconvinced. This is not to advocate the witless assumption that all our differences can be explained away by psychologizing puberty and menopause. That would be both bad psychology and bad theology. But if there really are some new and different things under the sun, they will be so for all of us. They will cause problems for all of us, they will alter perceptions for all of us, and they will change the shape of the quest for all of us whether we are prepared to acknowledge it or not. As a consequence, my comments will be about my own sense of the contemporary spiritual quest at least as often as they will concern the metaphysical gropings of today's youth.

Underlying our many and excruciating problems of war, race, and the maldistribution of wealth, power, and services, there are some profound shifts taking place that impinge heavily on the realm of the spirit. What we believe, how we believe, and even why we believe are all being subjected to serious and continual challenges. Perhaps by now we all have had the experience of having our view of something rearranged without our really being aware of it. Or, the pressure to form new understandings comes so fast and so repeatedly that our most recent mental pictures hardly have time to fall into place before we must construct new ones. Sometimes the pace of it all seems so overwhelming as to make reality itself a questionable proposition. If you have had such experiences, you too have been touched by these profound shifts. You may or may not be aware of the extent of the spiritual crisis into which they have propelled us, but you have felt something of the confusion and frustration they can produce.

It is with the young, inevitably, that the shock waves of serious perceptual change hit bottom. Their defenses are less set, and their major occupation is physiological, psychological, and intellectual development. And so, when the cultural process is shifting and uncertain and compounded by being conflict-ridden, they will feel and react to this with a peculiar force. In this sense they can become, and I think are today, weathervanes for us all. Whether they are or have been able to construct more satisfactory or enduring ways of responding to life as we are discovering it is surely open to question and remains for time to tell.

As one who has been both participant and observer in the current upheaval, I have been forced to acknowledge that, variegated and bizarre as it often is, the response of the young has kept me aware of the reality of the pain and danger we are all in. Some very important and binding myths have been shattered beyond repair; others have been shaken so much that their truth is hardly recognizable. In such a situation, winnowing out the good, the true, and the beautiful, as it were, is a distressing but necessary work. To use a biblical metaphor, it seems to be a time of harvest, and there are wheat and tares in all of our fields. But the threshing must and will go on, and it behooves us both to submit to this and to pay attention to the separation process. There is no other way to find out what is going to be kept and what is going to be discarded.

To focus this discussion I will take three aspects of human understanding whose development has sharply modified our sense of reality. When we are threatened with such modifications, we feel threatened in our very being. These three are not the sum of things causing our spiritual problems. But, because they run so deep and show so many faces, they are worth our serious consideration. The three are rationalism, pluralism, and relativism.

So many people have defended or attacked rationalism that one hesitates even to broach the subject again. Its benefit to humanity in delivering people from crippling superstitions and in ordering experience into more autonomous and controllable states is thoroughly documented and generally accepted. So too are many of its excesses, the most notable of which are its tendency to separate us from our feelings, sometimes at the expense of our humanity if not our sanity, and its assumption that mystery has been or will be banished from life. The truly wise have known that there is no necessary contradiction between the rational and the mysterious, or between reason and passion. Mystery is always there at the center of our existence, a mystery that beckons us and seeks to be known. Rationality is the name of the passion to know. But the predominant cultural tendency has been to confuse the issue by separating the two. In the process of separation, reason has been elevated to a kind of preeminence that has turned out to be more misleading than helpful. The mode of holiness in the rational religious scene is objectivity. The dispassionate analysis and synthesis that is the hallmark both of the academy and of the efficient organization generally is the outcome of this development. But it has brought with it unforeseen and sometimes grotesque distortions. The intractable and often unconscious human need to hold allegiances is sidestepped, suppressed, or ignored. The refusal of the intelligentsia to make, or even worse to acknowledge, value commitments is not perceived as a satisfactory response to the bourgeoisie thundering about a morality that is all too readily purchased by wealth or manipulated by power. The state of being value-free, so far from being regarded as beatific, has been increasingly seen as the tawdry prize of suborned pedagogues. It issues in the think tank whose members blithely solve problems the answers to which involve the destruction of an incredible amount of human life and achievement. This dominance of thinking without feeling, as it were, produced a huge spasm of its counterpart of feeling without thinking. In the present scene, why not try *I Ching* or astrology? Better to let the cast of a lot, or the stars, control your destiny than helpless sages, avaricious commercial interests, or bellicose politicians. Or, if the present system won't rationalize, or won't deliver the promised equity, try another one, preferably one which has clearly stated moral imperatives. Marx and Mao may be no better comprehended than, say, Jefferson, but they are ready at hand, full of the power to shock and enrage us with respect to our dominant interests and, cunningly enough, our dominant values.

The picture I present may be liable to the accusation of concentrating on the extremes. But they are extremes whose very powerful effects have been felt throughout our society. And even where they have not prevailed, they have left many of us in a badly confused and frustrated state, caught not between culture and counter-culture, but between absurdity and counter-absurdity, with any resemblance to culture being largely accidental.

Until we learn to strike some new balance between our reason and our emotions, I do not see any real progress in building a community fit for human beings. And until we are willing to attend seriously to the crisis situation in our values and valuing processes, I do not see how we can achieve any balance. Self-evident truth, the kind of truth from which values arise, is notoriously slippery and difficult material with which to deal. But we cannot continue to avoid the reality of this aspect of life. Leaving it to blind faith or to benign neglect as we have done has produced much of our present confusion. In a kind of gigantic cultural double-bind, we have ignored or denied the basis for ethics and at the same time threatened to lay waste the world in the interests of a particular brand of morality. It is not a rational dilemma, and it should not come as such a surprise that the reaction of the young frequently contains an unreasonable ring. An anonymous saying has it that you cannot reason people out of something that they were not reasoned into in the first place. We have reached the point where only occasional jolts of irrationality will shock us into changing our behavior.

It is not the failure of reason but of a particular configuration of rationalism that has caused us so much grief. We have not and cannot banish mystery from life, and we cannot live without understanding ourselves as creatures who live by myths which underlie and give shape to values. Anyone or anything that purports to deny this has to be labeled as a deceiver. Whether they are lucid about it, or confused or in despair, that is what I often hear from the young.

Another perceptual mode that has brought confusion along with its truth is pluralism. Whether in matters of religion or politics or economics or general behavior, pluralism holds that it is or ought to be possible for several models to exist side by side at the same time. It is the age-old problem of the one and the many, but the prevailing thrust is in the direction of the many. The development of pluralism was and is an entirely necessary step in the breakaway of human beings from oppressive systems of religious and political governance that are not just suffocating but lethal in their demands of uniformity. Pluralism is the actual content of the ideal of freedom. Whether in the laissez-faire life of "do your own thing" or the laissez-faire economics of free-enterprise commerce, we are persuaded that, to be fulfilled, we must be free to choose that which best suits us. The strength of our training and experience in this regard tells, in that we feel that our instinctive horror of monopoly must prevail over our equally instinctive fascination with it. It tells in our basic insistence that it is dangerous, if not wrong, to demand anything that smacks of the standardization of human conscience. Our deep commitment to pluralism makes us suspicious of systems and systematizers, and tears away at every effort, whether individual or collective, to "get it together."

And yet we have also and equally to deal with the indisputable fact that life is lived together with other human beings. We have to deal with the fact that this life together needs ordering as well as choice. Here again at the other end of the spectrum we feel that our instinctive horror of anarchism must prevail over our instinctive fascination with it.

The task of striking a useful balance in these matters can be incredibly difficult. The difficulty is compounded by the fact that the balance we do achieve quite properly may be short-lived. "New occasions teach new duties" runs the line from the old hymn. Unfortunately we are not usually ready to take that lyric seriously. But that does not mean that life is going to let us alone. For all its frenetic repetitiveness, Alvin Toffler's book *Future Shock* points up quite clearly that we are well into an era of metamorphosis which overtaxes our capacities for change in perceptions. The future, in the form of new and unfolding discoveries, more extended and instantaneous communication, and a mobility undreamed of a few short generations ago is coming at us so fast that we can hardly assimilate it. The tastemakers, hawking their wares and images at us incessantly, only confuse the issue further. We get so we cannot tell the difference between substantive change and cosmetic rearrangement.

In the midst of such a maelstrom we are often tempted to search for or construct an overarching something to which we can give our allegiance, and receive our security in return. Patriotism, dope, science, and "power to the people" are samples of that by which we hope to avoid being overwhelmed by choice. But as this short list itself suggests, there is no avoiding or turning back on pluralism. Its seeds are too firmly embedded in our experience. No matter how much trouble it causes us, the growing acceptance of a pluralistic outlook has provided us or our ancestors too much in the way of deliverance from social, religious, and political tyrannies for us to renounce it now.

And so we must go on trying to work out new or more satisfactory conventions to handle the inevitable clashes that develop along the interface of our choices. My style and your style, my party and your party are bound to collide sooner or later. We cannot and should not hope to avoid that. One of the myths that has been broken is that the mandate of heaven belongs to any one style or system or hero. The mandate of heaven is given by God to the human community to work out parities of style which affirm the diversities as well as the unity of life. Human beings need psychic or, if you will, spiritual territory as surely as they need spatial. To be sure, this makes the task of parity-setting more difficult, but it is dangerous and ultimately impossible to ignore spiritual needs. Historically the church (and this is a besetting difficulty of religious establishments) got into trouble, among other reasons, for asserting that spiritual affairs were of a higher nature and therefore more important than the material. As the untruth of this proposition became more and more apparent, the response of the church all too often has been to practice spiritual extortion on its adherents. The result has been a steady discrediting not only of the church, but of the spiritual realm as well. The ensuing dominance of emphasis on physical well-being, while badly needed in this materially lopsided world, has left a vacuum which is being felt more severely, and being filled with all manner of things from sorcery through meditation techniques to the Jesus freaks. But that is again the point. There will be a diversity of styles for a diversity of needs. Perhaps it is not so much a case of trying but of being forced to work out conventions which allow us to live more comfortably with one another in our differences. Even when we give ourselves to ever new forms of imperialism, these differences will continue to crop up. This bane to our monomania gives rise to some grotesque and chaotic possibilities but, on balance, it is better to suffer that than the process of being turned into so many puppets in superstar reviews.

The third development that is causing a great deal of spiritual havoc with its success is the steady encroachment of theories of relativity, probability, and indeterminacy on all aspects of our understanding of life. The homely old truth that life is an uncertain and transient affair is ever more demonstrably true. Despite, or along with, the piety summed up in the ancient Catholic motto, *Sic transit gloria mundi,* were deeply held opinions about perfect realities, unchanging substances, or absolute laws. Such opinions cannot hold together against the thrust of our experimentation and discoveries. Acknowledging that it is arbitrary to pick times or persons, still let us say that from Darwin through Einstein to the present, our picture and experience not only of the physical universe, but of human culture, human history, and human behavior has undergone radical rearrangement. As a result, it has become impossible to cling to any notions of fixed or absolute categories by which we may know or gauge our experience. Life is apparently more protean and dynamic than our ancestors could possibly have realized. I say apparently because the uncertainty principle applies to all unqualified statements including the statement, "There are no such things as absolutes." Paradoxically, as we have been forced to give up our more static pictures of reality, we have come across an expansion of knowledge that seems, at times, almost too much for us to handle. Despite the problems posed by this overload, the very fact of the knowledge explosion persuades us that our departures from past beliefs are warranted.

The sweeping transformation of outlook which we are undergoing brings with it two powerful and contrasting senses. On the one hand, the sweep of relativism brings with it a sense of deliverance from all closed systems which, however much they might promise, always conclude with a tragic imprisonment of human potential. On the other hand, there emerges a tremendous sense of deprivation. If everything is relative, we have lost or are threatened with the loss of having anything discernible in common with each other. Yeats struck a prophetic note about this in his poem "The Second Coming." [1] The loss of center which he notes and of a sense of having anything in common is reflected in our terrible ordeals within ourselves and our communities today. Every person for himself or herself, every system for itself, and, because we have few, if any, agreed-upon bases for satisfying conflicting claims, persons and communities come apart at the seams or club each other to death in the name of self-protection. We may wonder, again with Yeats:

> . . . What rough beast, its hour come round at last,
> Slouches towards Bethlehem to be born.[2]

As I indicated earlier, these events and their attendant traumata are not the property of the young alone. They belong to all of us. The era through which we are living has been described by several commentators as a period of fundamental transition for humanity. It has been likened to the shift from hunting and fishing to agricultural lifestyle that took place at the dawn of civilization.[3] Whether or not such sweeping assessments ring true, it is hard to deny that what we are going through institutes a set of major developments of the human race.

If this is so, then perhaps we should not be so dismayed

to find that the passage brings with it an acute identity crisis. Just as individuals can experience great travail in self-definition at times of major transition, so too does the race. It is the kind of experience that drives us back to our origins, seeking to explain who we are and where we came from in hopes that we will learn something of where we are going. The current vogue of primitivism, so incongruous in a generation weaned on set theory, is a case in point. The reversion to, or fascination with, barter economy, occult religion, and tribal organization are others. Appalled by the apparent limitation of choice to plastic achievement (cf. *The Graduate*), overwhelmed by the capacity we have to be destructive both in war (even a "limited" war like Vietnam) and peace (the plunder of the environment), and daunted by the perception that the task ahead is of no less magnitude than building a new order of humanity, the prescience is at times almost too much to bear. These are problems and tasks that we are all aware of somewhere deep in our bones, but it is difficult to imagine that we would be as aware as we are without the prodding of the young. Whether their prodding has been born of confusion or clarity, and there has been a great deal of both, or whether the sheer weight of numbers emanating from the dramatic rise in birth rate from 1945 to 1953 is a major factor, we have not been able to ignore the signals. Painful as it may be, that has to be counted for the good.

1. William Butler Yeats, "The Second Coming," *Selected Poems and Two Plays of William Butler Yeats*, ed. by M. L. Rosenthal (New York: Collier Books, 1970), p. 91.

2. *Ibid.*

3. Kenneth Boulding, *Meaning of the 20th Century: The Great Transition* (New York: Harper & Row, 1967). William Irwin Thompson, *At the Edge of History* (New York: Harper & Row, 1971).

ROBERT N. BELLAH:

## No Direction Home—Religious Aspects of the American Crisis

Bob Dylan in one of his most powerful songs asks us how it feels "to be on our own" without direction home.[1] Obviously to most of us in America today it doesn't feel very good. It seems as though, almost without knowing when, we have lost the way. Thomas O'Dea[2] has recently likened our situation to one depicted by an earlier poet, Dante, in the opening lines of the "Inferno":

> In the middle of the journey of our life
> I came to my senses in a dark forest,
> for I had lost the straight path.

Dante at least knew where home was, even if he felt lost. For him God and Paradise were sure. We don't even know where home is; for us there is literally no direction home. There is an immense nostalgia and longing for home, for being at home, but our reality is an acute, radical homelessness.

Most Americans have never been at home in this land. This is not only because most of us are immigrants or the descendants of immigrants who have generation after generation continued to wander over the face of this continent. It is also because most of the founding fathers believed in some version of that religious tradition of which Dante was an earlier expression. For them this earth was only a temporary abode. They were to be in but not of this world. Their true home was their Father's house, and their Father was in heaven. This earth was simply the location of the long upward climb, the "Pilgrim's Progress," which was to end gloriously in heaven. Gradually, over the course of several centuries, that upward course has become truncated. The heavenly home in which it ends is a split level in suburbia supplied with all the latest electrical equipment. In this transition hope has become gradually overpowered by fear. One cannot really be at home in a house if one feels physically and morally unsure about one's possession of it, if one needs to purchase guns to defend it. As Max Weber pointed out nearly seventy years ago, the life lived in obedience to the heavenly Father when the heavenly Father has disappeared is an iron cage.[3] And what we can see even more clearly than Weber is that within the iron cage is an ever-accelerating treadmill.

It is the shattering of the myth of the sky home and the deepening disillusionment with the pseudo-home called success which gradually took its place that more than anything has precipitated our present crisis. Secular values first nurtured by the myth of the sky home have wrenched themselves loose and have set our society on a course of uncontrolled acceleration. Wealth and power, when they become ends in themselves, lead inevitably to the destruction of the natural environment, other weaker societies, the less privileged within our own society, and finally and inexorably to the destruction of those most fervently and successfully dedicated to them. As this has become increasingly clear there has occurred a massive revulsion against these dominant secular values, a convulsive reaction to the attack by those most committed to them, and so the collapse of that great consensus which has for long, though never so totally as the apologists have claimed, characterized American society.

Throughout human history in times of trouble when the common values are collapsing there has arisen a nostalgia for a former, better time. In the late twentieth century we see that old tendency in a somewhat new form. It has been common for the nostalgia to be directed toward an earlier phase of the same society, and there is some of that, or to a purely mythical golden age, and there is a good deal of that. What is new is the considerable historical and anthropological resources being utilized in the current nostalgic fantasies. What we see is nothing less than a paleolithic revival, and its hero is the one group of people who ever really felt at home in America, the American Indians.

The young Americans who have made what Thomas O'Dea calls "the great refusal," [4] that is, the refusal to enter the iron cage, have developed a new earth mysticism. They want to live with great simplicity and directness, as the Indians did, in an earth home or, in Gary Snyder's words, an Earth House Hold.[5] Phillis Harris in her poem "Furniture" [6] has beautifully captured the contrast between the old and the new visions:

> there are youngsters now
> younger than I, moving as nomads
> through the makeshift camping grounds
>
> who do not hope for what was
> expected: the catalog comforts
> of minor success
>
> nor do they imagine
> changelessness, that what they encounter
> remains
>
> whose parents
> in the suburbs, in the small
> midwestern towns

have set down heavy houses on the land
and filled them
with a weight of furnishings, & in a manner
held them down

but not their children: who dreamed of Indians
tracking.
& move lightly, from city
to city

exchanging
adornments; themselves the only
shelter they have found

But unlike these young people, most American Indians were not nomadic. They found long ago what our youth are still seeking. They were at home in their land, in the cosmos, in their bodies. Among the Pueblo Indians the kiva, the underground ceremonial chamber built into or near every pueblo, was itself a microcosm of the universe. The kiva "recapitulates in structural form" the "four-world universe" [7] of Pueblo mythology:

In the floor is a small hole, the *sipapu,* leading down into the first underworld. The floor level is the second world into which man emerged. The raised seating ledge represents the third world. And the ladder rises up to the roof opening, the fourth world to which man has climbed. . . .
  In the kiva, man is ever reminded that he lives in the whole of the immense and naked universe. And he is constantly made aware of the psychic, universal harmony which he must help to perpetuate by his ceremonial life.[8]

For the Navaho, who have no kivas, the hogan or ordinary dwelling has the same symbolic meaning as the Pueblo kiva. This is indeed being at home in the world.
  In contrast to the traditional American heroic image of

the Indian as solitary, self-reliant, and individualistic, the new image is more anthropologically informed, if still in part romantic. It is the Indian in organic harmony with himself, his communal society, and his natural environment. Not only the Indians but all the remnants of primitive and archaic culture and their survival in the form of heresies and sects in the great civilizations are celebrated in the new culture. Gary Snyder speaks of "a surfacing (in a specifically 'American' incarnation) of the Great Subculture which goes back as far perhaps as the late Paleolithic." [9] He sees this Great Subculture surviving in such forms as shamanism, witchcraft, Taoism, Tantrism, Sufism, and Gnosticism. Unlike the religions of the Sky Father, this tradition celebrates Nature as a mother. The sky religions emphasize the paternal, hierarchical, legalistic, and ascetic, whereas the earth tradition emphasizes the maternal, communal, expressive, and joyful aspects of existence. Whereas the sky religions see fathers, teachers, rulers, and gods exercising external control through laws, manipulation, or force, the earth tradition is tuned to cosmic harmonies, vibrations, and astrological influences. Socially the Great Subculture expresses itself not through impersonal bureaucracy or the isolated nuclear family but through collectives, communes, tribes, and large extended families. The contrast between the old American culture and the new Earth culture could hardly be more striking, but, as Philip Slater has pointed out, the two are not unrelated.[10] Each expresses what the other has repressed. Each has inner enemies on the other side; in fact every American is a mixture of both.

The recovery of mythical consciousness, of the archaic world-view, is one of the great achievements of modern scholarship. We need not be shocked that it has at last begun to have practical consequences, that the writings of Mircea Eliade are programming the patterns of life in rural hippie communes. Civilization has indeed been based on the repression of a great deal of human experience which is now being liberated. We have much to learn from the surviving primitive and archaic cultures and it is very late for us to become aware of it. Particularly for us in America the existence of intact Indian cultures like the Pueblos and the Navahos is an incomparable treasure. This battered remnant of a decimated people may yet provide the saving wisdom which will make possible our renewal.

Yet the simple abandonment of civilization, science, and technology in favor of a new tribalism is not a solution. If we have seen the fatal consequences of the degeneration of sky religions we cannot afford to overlook how constricting historically the rule of the Earth Mother has often been and how liberating at an earlier period was the role of the Sky Father. At its best the earth religion has been an elaborate dance giving expression to all the forces of the universe and to the role of each person in his society. But all too easily such patterns can harden. The divine cosmos turns out to be only a petty tribelet deifying itself and dominated by old men who oppose every innovation. Or the cosmic forces concentrate themselves in a divine king and the tribe becomes a predatory imperialist state. And our counter-culture has produced its share of despotic gurus and narrow-minded dogmas.

Under these circumstances the being at home so characteristic of the earth religions becomes not an image of life but of stagnation and death, and the sky father who calls one to leave home is the liberator. Moses was called to leave Egypt and lead his people to a new and more precarious home. He spent his days in wandering and died in the wilderness. Jesus too was a wanderer. The birds of the air have their nests and the foxes of the field their holes but the son of man has not where to lay his head. Buddha declared the world to be a burning house and called on his followers to take to the road with only a begging bowl in hand. In Japan to become a monk is to *shukke,* to leave home. In all these cases there is a home, but it is a sky home, kingdom of heaven, western paradise. The tension between this earth and the sky home generates unease, and often pressure for social change, for the greater realization of values in human society. This is the significance of prophetic religion, the achievements of which we forget at our peril when we reject the modern world too radically.

It is this restless tradition of the sky religion that lies behind the great experiment which is America, and which is still not without vitality. Not all Americans outside the counter-culture are materialistic robots. Many of them still live in the tension between this world and the kingdom of heaven. The original intention of the founders of America was that it become a place on this earth more like the kingdom of heaven. America was to be a city set on a hill, a home for the homeless and oppressed, a haven for the uprooted and the dispossessed. But prophetic religions have often made rather sharp distinctions between the chosen and the others. The irony is that this great new home for the homeless was itself based on a most massive forcible dispossession (of the Indians) and forcible uprooting (of Negro slaves). The great experiment was tainted with sin from the beginning and, as we know, has always been far from perfect. And yet even now it is far from devoid of energies for a new beginning.

But at the moment American society seems to be coming apart at the seams and neither the earth home nor the sky home are very comfortable places in which to dwell. In the midst of the collapse of our common beliefs and our division into ever-more-polarized groups, more and more of our people are encountering, as other peoples have before us, what Michael Novak has recently called "the experience of nothingness." [11] In this experience we find that the bottom has dropped out, that in the depth of the earth home and the sky home there is no home at all, that at the root of every belief is an absolute doubt and at the core of every self and every culture is absolute nothingness. And yet this radical and shattering experience is not ultimately an experience of despair. The powerful element of death in it is overcome by the possibility of rebirth. The experience of nothingness exposes man as in some deep and not wholly conscious way the creator of his own myths, and that is not only a frightening but also an immensely liberating experience.

Of course the experience of nothingness is not new in human history. It is one of the great archetypal religious experiences, like the encounter with the Earth Mother or the Sky Father. It was perhaps first experienced by a Paleolithic shaman. In any case it is reported, especially by mystics, in all the great traditions. Novak himself points to St. John of the Cross and his image of the dark night and the happy night. There is no religion that has meditated more deeply on nothingness and emptiness than Buddhism and no culture more influenced by such meditation than the Japanese. When the experience of nothingness first burst upon modern Europe in the nineteenth century it was frightening and shattering, as the word "nihilism" implies, because there were few resources in the available tradition to help in dealing with it. Perhaps now in the twentieth century when the experience becomes ever more commonplace we can draw on the Japanese tradition to help us cope with it.

The Japanese, especially after the devastating experiences which they underwent in their early Middle Ages, developed what might be called an art of insecurity. They glorified the fleeting and the transient—the cherry blossoms which quickly fall, the dew which rapidly evaporates —as the truest expressions of the nature of reality. In the culture which Zen Buddhism had much to do with shaping, it was precisely in poverty and loneliness that one might most readily know one's Buddha nature. Among other things the Japanese developed in the haiku a poetic art of the utmost brevity devoted precisely to revealing the ultimate emptiness in the minutiae of everyday life. Just to give one example appropriate to our theme:[12]

*Furusato mo/ima wa karine/wataridori.*

My old home
Now but a night's lodging;
Birds of passage.

The Japanese, it seems, have gone far to make the no home comfortable, or to create a no-home home. This too is dangerous, for if the experience of nothingness becomes too comfortable it can become constricting and lose its potential for creativity. Still, for us the Japanese experience is very instructive. In particular we might explore the suggestion of Nishida Kitarō, Japan's greatest modern philosopher, who combined the vocabulary of Zen Buddhism and Western philosophy, that nothingness, *mu*, or absolute nothingness, *zettai-teki mu*, might be thought of as a place, a topos, or in Japanese, *basho*. In such a place "the individual lives through dying," that is, he affirms himself through negating himself.[13]

Of course we have numerous American cultural expressions of the experience of nothingness. In an earlier generation there was Thomas Wolfe's *You Can't Go Home Again*. One of Bob Dylan's most moving songs, "Desolation Row,"[14] is an almost pure expression of the experience of nothingness, and the phrase from another song that provides my title is a beautiful example of the simultaneous emptiness and fullness of that experience, and in turn suggests Shakespeare's line: "And nothing brings me all things."

A number of recent commentators on the American cultural scene have described it as bifurcated, as a culture and a counter-culture, an old culture and a new culture, a house divided, half-slave, half-free.[15] My distinction between those seeking a sky home and those seeking an earth home is roughly parallel to that of these other commentators. I have also tried to delineate another archetypal religious mode, the experience of nothingness or no home, which is increasingly affecting Americans on both sides of the cultural divide. But I do not see the third mode as a category on the same level as the other two producing a triple rather than a double division of our national culture. Rather, following Paul Tillich, I would see the experience of nothingness as the dimension of depth in both the others. As such it does not offer simply another degree of fracture, but the possibility, however remote, of reconciliation and rebirth. For the experience of nothingness does not involve rejection of the other experiences. Once one has felt the ultimate emptiness of the sky home and the earth home, one can still dwell in those houses and with much less danger of stagnation, constriction, arrogance, and

pride. Indeed the experience of the place of absolute nothingness, because it is continuously self-negating, makes it
possible to live in many houses, in many mansions. It also
makes possible the recovery of twofold vision, the appre-
hension of old myth in new ways, and the creation of new
myth. It may help provide a key to the genuine pluralism
which we have sought in America but which so far has always eluded us.

The starting point for a genuine pluralism has to be the
realization that the American tradition, the Western tradition, or even the biblical tradition provides insufficient resources to meet the desperate problems that beset us. Rich
as those traditions are and much as we still need to study
them, if we cling obstinately to them alone we will be
guilty of a narrow and probably ultimately self-destructive
parochialism. We must be able to embrace the experience
of the rootedness of the American Indians, the uprooted-
ness of the Blacks, the emptiness of the Asians, not out of
some charitable benevolence but because our own traditions are simply not enough. Cultural defensiveness will be
fatal. If we are to survive on this earth, we must embrace
the entire human tradition, make all of it, potentially at
least, available to our imagination.

Because of the absolutism that is so much a part of
Western philosophical and religious thought, what I have
just said may conjure up some notion of what is usually
called syncretism: some fluid pudding in which all of the
world's religions and cultures will lose their integrity in the
general swill. But it is precisely the experience of nothingness that can allow us to expand our cultural horizons in-
definitely without losing the integrity of the several visions.
Let me turn to the words of Herbert Fingarette to help explain how this can be. He says:

It is the special fate of modern man that he has a "choice" of spiritual visions. The paradox is that although each requires complete commitment for complete viability, we can today generate a context in which we see that no one of them is the sole vision. Thus we must learn to be naive but undogmatic. That is, we must take the vision as it comes and trust ourselves to it, naively, as reality. Yet we must retain an openness to experience such that the dark shadows deep within one vision are the mute stubborn messengers waiting to lead us to a new light and a new vision.[16]

Those dark shadows within every vision are precisely the emptiness and the nothingness that we have spoken of. They deprive every vision of its absoluteness, though not of its integrity. Fingarette uses our central motif, home and being at home, to shed light on this aspect of the problem as well:

We must not ignore the fact that in the last analysis, commitment to a specific orientation outweighs catholicity of imagery. One may be a sensitive and seasoned traveler, at ease in many places, but one must have a home. Still, we can be intimate with those we visit, and while we may be only travelers and guests in some domains, there are our hosts who are truly at home. Home is always home for someone; but there is no Absolute Home in general.[17]

There is no Absolute Home. Once again we see that in the depths of every home is its own provisionality, its own emptiness, its own no home.

Let us consider the critical and constructive implications of starting from the no-home home, the "place" of absolute nothingness. The pretensions of all self-sufficient institutions are exposed. Michael Novak shows us how when he says:

I also wish to show that even the most solid and powerful social institutions, though they may imprison us, impoverish us,
or kill us, are fundamentally mythical structures designed to
hold chaos and formlessness at bay: they are more like
dreams than like reality. The experience of nothingness . . .
dissolves the pragmatic solidity of the American way of life.[18]

Taking nothing for granted we are thus freed to think of
drastic solutions for drastic problems. As ever-larger segments of the population share the experience of nothingness it will become possible to make the needed changes.
Not that it will be easy, for there are many more threatened than liberated by our present predicament. These are
the people who easily adopt such slogans as "America,
love it or leave it" and "Shape up or ship out."

In dealing with such people we may be more effective if
we remember that their slogans and their ideologies are
"designed to hold chaos and formlessness at bay." In this,
however limited and defensive their beliefs, they are like
the rest of us. It is well to remember that the split-level
suburban home serves, in however emasculated a form, as
a kiva of sorts for its occupants. It is an island of security
in a chaotic sea, and however strongly we may need to
criticize its limitations, it does serve some human function.

In the end, of course, particular political programs are
not dictated by religious insights alone. The religious insight may give us the vision of the society we want, but attaining that society is a matter of careful social analysis
and hard work. The experience of nothingness, however, is
just as helpful in judging alternative political strategies as
it is in unmasking the pretensions of established institutions. A political program, even though it uses the rhetoric
of liberation and socialism, that promises to lead only to a
somewhat more equalitarian and possibly more efficient

iron cage is no solution. A collective split-level mentality that argues for accelerating socialist GNP and proliferating socialist heavy technology is not necessarily better than an individualistic split-level mentality. All political programs require rational analysis. But one rather direct criterion for judging a program is the character of the people espousing it. Revolutionaries who in their own lives do not embody the future cannot bring it.

Another critical contribution of the experience of nothingness is the awareness that our present crisis goes deeper than politics. It concerns the very nature of man. What availeth a revolution in property relations if there is no revolution in ego boundaries? This deeper revolution is calling into question those profound differentiations and specializations upon which civilization rests, not only in the social division of labor but in the inner economy of the psyche. The boundaries that more advanced societies have fixed between the conscious and the unconscious, between the spirit and the body, and between an individual and all that is around him are not eternal. Many see only chaos in tampering with those boundaries, and certainly the dangers are great. In particular the distinction between impulse and discipline cannot simply be abandoned. Structure and form are part of the essence of human existence. "But," as Norman O. Brown has put it, "the path to that ultimate reunification of ego and body is not a dissolution but a strengthening of the human ego. The human ego would have to become strong enough to die." [19] The experience of nothingness with its protean ability for self-negation, for continuous death and rebirth, may provide the basis for that ultimate reunification of what civilization has too long sundered. It may be possible once again to be at home in our bodies and in our cosmos, as primitive men have been, but this time consciously, and aware that this being at home too is provisional and never absolute.

This hope would be forlorn were it not already partially and fragmentarily being realized. There are communes, intentional communities, underground and experimental churches, and religious collectives that are already establishing themselves, like kibbutzim, in the desert of our nothingness, already trying to live in entirely new ways. There are also individual mystics and prophets who, like scouts and guides in the wilderness, are reconnoitering the broken terrain that lies ahead. It is not yet clear which of these attempts is on the right track. But we have moved beyond words into experiment and practice.

I think we must expect to live for some time, perhaps for a long time, in tension and uncertainty. There will be many groups and many tendencies, some devoted to conserving some element from the past, some to experimenting with the future. I neither expect nor hope for some final showdown, some Armageddon, between the two halves of a polarized America. Such a showdown could only result in massive repression, whoever won. The experience of nothingness should help us tolerate the tension and complexity involved in moving toward a more open and a more just society.

The experience of nothingness certainly does not mean the rejection of our heritage, biblical or American. Indeed that experience is deep within our heritage. It is the experience of exile, of Christ crucified, which must be taken with absolute seriousness before there can be any talk of return, or resurrection. It is the experience of a society which rejects all absolutisms, whether of man, class, or dogma. We do not need to reject our past, but as with every generation, we need to rediscover it for ourselves. And the present cultural situation allows us to ask questions that have not been asked for a long time. It allows us, children of Protestant literalism and enlightenment rationalism that we are, to consider traditions of mysticism and negative theology that have flourished more in the Hasidic movement and the Eastern churches than in the Western religious bodies, traditions that emphasize a joyous union with God more than law and theology alone. And the present cultural situation allows us, children of free enterprise that we are, to consider the possibility of a democratic and humane socialism as an alternative to the rabid and cruel competition that still governs so much of our lives.

The experience of nothingness is not an alternative. It is not another home. Instead it gives us back all the homes that we have lost, only now without clinging or attachment. It puts us beyond optimism and pessimism. We need neither the optimism of Agnew about what is right with America nor the optimism of Charles Reich about turning America green. We can accept what each day brings as sufficient thereto. We know that we must never be so much at home that we forget that we are also on the road, traveling, and that we may at any time find a mansion more marvelous than any we have found before.

We can be at home on the earth, on that "old chaos of the sun" as Wallace Stevens called it. With Stevens we can with joy observe

> Deer walk on our mountains, and the quail
> Whistle about us their spontaneous cries;
> Sweet berries ripen in the wilderness;
> And, in the isolation of the sky,
> At evening, casual flocks of pigeons make
> Ambiguous undulations as they sink,
> Downward to darkness, on extended wings.[20]

But because we are conscious and because we have the power of the imagination ("How high that highest candle lights the dark") we can be at home in the sky too:

> We make a dwelling in the evening air,
> In which being there together is enough.[21]

And all this because we know the nothing of which Norman O. Brown has so beautifully spoken:

The world annihilated, the destruction of illusion. The world is the veil we spin to hide the void. The destruction of what never existed. The day breaks, and the shadows flee away.

The absence; a withdrawal, leaving vacant space, or void, to avoid the plenum of omnipresence. The god who, mercifully, does not exist.

A void, an opening for us, to leave the place where we belong; a road into the wilderness; for exodus, exile. The Proletariate has no fatherland, and the son of man no place to lay his head. Be at home nowhere.[22]

1. Bob Dylan, "Like a Rolling Stone," from Bob Dylan, "Highway 61 Revisited," Columbia LP record.

2. Thomas F. O'Dea, "Significant 20th Century Transformations of Thought in America," paper delivered at the American Sociological Association meetings, September, 1970, p. 3.

3. Max Weber, *The Protestant Ethic and the Spirit of Capitalism*, trans. Talcott Parsons (New York: Scribners, 1958), p. 181.

4. *Op. cit.,* p. 10.

5. Gary Snyder, *Earth House Hold* (New York: New Directions, 1969).

6. In Sara Hannum and John Terry Chase, *To Play Man Number One* (New York: Atheneum, 1969), p. 32.

7. Frank Waters, *Masked Gods: Navaho and Pueblo Ceremonialism* (New York: Ballantine Books, 1970), p. 170.

8. *Ibid.,* p. 171.

9. *Op. cit.,* p. 104.

10. Philip E. Slater, *The Pursuit of Loneliness* (Boston: Beacon, 1970), chap. 1, particularly p. 28.

11. Michael Novak, *The Experience of Nothingness* (New York: Harper & Row, 1970).

12. R. H. Blyth, tr., *Haiku,* Vol. 4 (Tokyo-Hokuseido Press, 1965), p. 69. The poem is by Kyorai (1651–1704). I have altered Blyth's translation.

13. Nishida Kitarō, *Fundamental Problems of Philosophy*, trans. David A. Dilworth (Sophia University Press, 1970), p. 49. The original was written in 1933.

14. Also on "Highway 61 Revisited."

15. Theodore Roszak, *The Making of a Counter Culture* (Garden City: Doubleday, 1969); Philip E. Slater, *op. cit.;* Charles Reich, "The Greening of America," *New Yorker,* September 26, 1970; Robert Jay Lifton, *History and Human Survival* (New York: Random House, 1970).

16. Herbert Fingarette, *The Self in Transformation* (New York: Harper Torchbooks, 1963), p. 236.

17. *Ibid.,* p. 237.

18. *Op. cit.,* p. 1.

19. Norman O. Brown, *Life against Death* (Middletown, Conn.: Wesleyan University Press, 1959), p. 292.

20. Wallace Stevens, *Collected Poems* (New York: Knopf, 1955), p. 70.

21. *Ibid.,* p. 524.

22. Norman O. Brown, *Love's Body* (New York: Vintage Book, 1968), pp. 261–262.

N.B. Professor Bellah's paper is his Dudleian Lecture delivered, November 18, 1970, at Harvard University Divinity School, Cambridge, Massachusetts.

## Days after Block Island

The Block Island meeting was not what I'd expected. For three months since then I've tried to write this paper, expand on the ideas I presented there in abbreviated form—the spiritual quest of the young. Now, a month past deadline I'm angry. Angry at myself, angry that the Block Island conference was so much intellectual gamesmanship, angry at the bullshit, angry at the liberalism that sucked me into its mystification of the issues and away from plain speech and telling it like it is.

Now this pours out of the mind and the typewriter—like a diary of anger and a diary of these three months.

*George Jackson:* We were in Los Angeles—the Echo Park chicano district—when we got the news, "George Jackson's just been killed!" The words hit us like a slug in the pit of the stomach.

There's a feeling we get at times like these, that losing count of the dead sisters and brothers is like losing the struggle itself. We remembered King and Malcolm X, all those bloodied Panthers like Bobby Hutton, Mark Clark, and Fred Hampton, James Rector, Kent, Jonathan Jackson the fierce man-child, those in exile, those in prison, those gone underground. The strong urgent necessity to remember, to tell our children, not to forget, never to let the killers forget either.

*San Quentin:* George Jackson, black warrior, Soledad Brother, political prisoner and poet, was murdered at San Quentin on August 21, 1971. "They've pushed me over the line from which there can be no retreat. I know that they will not be satisfied until they've pushed me out of this existence altogether." [1]

With our baby, Jeremiah, in the back-pack, we drove to San Quentin to join five hundred demonstrators outside the gates. We never got to the gates. The road was blocked by police cars, highway patrol, and two dozen shotgun-bearing pigs. The demonstration took place right there, on the freeway offramp. The chants were clear: "Stop the torture, open the gates" and "Three pigs dead is not enough."

Six months old and your first demonstration, Jeremiah Bethune. Time to remember your namesake, Norman Bethune, Mao's revolutionary Canadian physician. Time to remember your already-victory over piggery which was your birth, a year after the Berkeley pigs assaulted your mother, and we feared we would lose you, and beat up your father. Start yelling Jeremiah! Prophesy doom on this house. Now they've killed George Jackson. Melinda and I make quick plans on which way to run with the baby if they assault us all again, here on the offramp.

A week later the George L. Jackson Assault Squad of the Black Liberation Army walked into the Ingleside Station in San Francisco and calmly blew a sergeant away. A Bank of America was bombed, and a parking lot of State of California cars in Berkeley was firebombed. Three more bombs went off in the Department of Corrections offices in San Francisco, San Mateo, and Sacramento. The Weathermen claimed two of them.[2]

We are at war, George said, a "war without terms."

*San Francisco:* On August 26 a pretrial hearing for Fleeta Drumgo and John Clutchette, the remaining Soledad Brothers, was held in the courtroom of Superior Court Judge Carl Allen. Fleeta and John limped into court. The attorneys explained to the judge that the men were being beaten and tortured in Quentin, and that both brothers feared for their lives if they were returned. When the judge said that he had no evidence to support this, Fleeta took off his shirt and showed the courtroom cigarette burns on the back of his neck. He cried to the judge, "You're gonna kill me anyway. Why don't you just kill me now . . ."

Mrs. Maxwell, Clutchette's mother, began sobbing out loud in the courtroom. She was ordered removed. With no warning about twenty armed Tactical Squad Police, who had been waiting for this opportunity, burst into the courtroom swinging riot sticks. We watched TV as they beat and clubbed every black man, woman, and child in the courtroom, finally remembering to pull the doors shut behind them to finish the job, so the cameramen couldn't film the rest of it. When they finished, they opened the doors and drove everybody out. Mrs. Maxwell was hysterical, two pregnant women were beaten, two brothers were bloodied beyond recognition, everyone was screaming, sobbing, clubbed.

A few days later the courts indicted our friend Steve Bingham on five counts of murder, a charge trumped up, like those against Angela, on nonevidence. He was the last lawyer to see George Jackson. We got a call telling us to expect pig raids at all the collectives. Later that very afternoon, the pigs showed up at our house. "Yes, you have the right address," Melinda said. "No, we did not report a robbery." Are they serious?

*Attica:* We listened to the reporter interview an ex-inmate of Quentin. The press asked him, "If George was murdered, then how do you explain the dead guards?" The black responded, "They will sacrifice anybody, even their mother, to make it look good." Preposterous? Attica proved him right.

Fifteen hundred prisoners liberated Cell Block D on September 10, 1971. Attica, 85 percent black and Puerto Rican, all guards white, taking thirty-four hostages, prisoners of war armed with billy clubs, fists, imagination, and rage. "When you don't give a damn, you don't have nothing to give up but your life." Outside, hundreds of state troopers, sheriffs' deputies, guards, riot guns at the ready, and helicopters overhead.

The *New York Times*, bewildered: "Just why the uprising took place remained unclear." It's all too clear—read the demands. Oswald concedes to twenty-eight of the demands dealing with human rights and survival needs, but refuses to consider the demands for free passage to a nonimperialistic country and intervention by federal authorities. Rockefeller-Pilate washes his hands. Refuses amnesty.

Monday morning the massacre. Thirty-four revolutionary brothers killed by invading troopers, and nine hostages too—shot by the pigs, by Oswald, by Rockefeller. The exinmate was right, they will sacrifice anybody.

When the press interviewed one brother and asked for his name, the brother answered, "My name is Attica, I am all of us."

George Jackson had written, "There are still some Blacks here who consider themselves criminals—but not many. Believe me my friend, with the time and incentive that these brothers have to read, study, think, you will find no class or category more aware, more embittered, desperate, or dedicated to the ultimate remedy—revolution. The most dedicated, the best of our kind—you'll find them in the Folsoms, San Quentins, and Soledads."[3] And in Attica.

*Santa Rita:* I drove for forty-five minutes through the eastern part of the county to Santa Rita Rehabilitation Center, where People's Park demonstrators were tortured in the hot sun by Sheriff Madigan and his thugs, to visit David, a Free Church staff member, now in prison for six months. We all miss him and love him. He'd been in two weeks. We wondered how he would make it. He had heard only fragmentary reports of Quentin and Attica. I filled him in on all I could hold in my head. Later he wrote us:

Things go better for me here—as I learn more, I am less alienated from this environment. Doing time is a subtle and delicate art. Its masters display an exquisite grace; an ability to endure sanely persecution without sacrificing either dignity or sensitivity; a profound strength, not in the bourgeois individualistic sense of invulnerability, but in the preservation of compassion and revolutionary consciousness in spite of everything. I feel the massacre at Attica like an open wound. I'm already so sick of eulogizing the martyrs of the revolution, and we've hardly begun to resist. Even realizing the demonic capabilities (e.g., My Lai, Auschwitz, etc.) I am shocked anew by each atrocity. I am learning how to more clearly and less impulsively recognize imperatives—to think tactically—to discipline myself to function when necessary with cold, calculating precision, without sacrificing sensitivity. Nixon's prisons taught Timothy Leary to speak of "armed Love," China's impelled Ho Chi Minh to say, "Calamity has tempered and hardened me/ And turned my mind to steel." This vision develops not out of bitterness, or hatred, but of reason and its active expression, an unemotional confidence.

*Berkeley:* I testified this month at a City-sponsored hearing on drug abuse in Berkeley, moderated by a prominent physician who, having worked at the Free Clinic, ought to have known better. When I was finished telling his committee that the way to deal with drug abuse was to begin seriously treating the causes of alienation, like the war and the draft and racism, he set down his gavel and gave a speech in which he claimed that the war had nothing to do with drug abuse.

It blew my mind. Nixon's junkie army is all over Telegraph Avenue. Strung-out veterans on junk. It's all over Vietnam too. And that's saying nothing about all the other kids shooting up their stuff, just hot in from those subsidized super-pushers, the warlords.

*First Congregational:* The First Congregational Church of Berkeley is one of the most uptight churches in town. They, along with others, have consistently refused to give Free Church and other movement organizations any space in their extremely unused buildings. But we have, for a time at least, infiltrated First Congo. You see, their janitor is a Free Churcher, and so every other week we gather in his apartment in the bowels of First Congo, to celebrate the Freedom Meal.

This week about eight of us were there. Some brought bread and wine, others contributed spaghetti, others salad. It began like our men's and women's liberation groups, with self-criticism. We went around the circle, in no particular order, criticizing ourselves for chauvinism, counter-revolutionary attitudes, sloth, not being upfront, oppressing someone. When we were done, someone read from Luke and Matthew about Jesus washing feet to give us an example of his way of serving the people instead of exploiting them. Then we passed around a basin of water and all washed our hands (and our brother's blood) for dinner.

We set a table in the middle of the room, and people presented their gifts of food and drink. "If you are bringing your gift to the altar, and there remember that your sister or brother has something against you, leave your gift there; go and first be reconciled to your sister or brother, and then come back and offer your gift." So we criticized each other. Not just to get things off our chests, but as a revolutionary discipline. When this was done, we passed around the kiss of peace, and sat down to eat.

Halfway through dinner the bread was broken and we were reminded that Jesus did this with his collective and that to eat it here has special meaning: it is like signing a revolutionary manifesto, like joining the Movement again. To do it lightly means trouble, because it is solidarity with your sisters and brothers that you are eating in lightly. Eating it lightly, you condemn yourself to your own ego-tripping or elitism, because you betray the collective Body.

Then the wine was poured—"this is the Constitution of a New Society in my Blood." After dinner we poured more wine and drank toasts, responding to each with the amen of "Right on." Our toasts were to our brother David in Santa Rita, to the freedom of Angela, the Soledad Brothers, the Berrigans, and all political prisoners; they were for our Switchboard and its growing political consciousness; for the junkies we met that week, for the several couples just married, and a special toast to Corey Hue, our new-born comrade. And there were more. Late in the night, the age-old revolutionary meal over, we went home.

*(415)* *549-0649:* That number gets you the Berkeley Switchboard, the hub and primary energy center of the Free Church. I remember the days, in 1967, when the Free Church and Switchboard was an everybody-do-your-own-thing hippie haven on the Avenue. But times have

changed. The flower children didn't just fade away: they were cut, beaten, stomped, busted, and brutalized into the pavement.

This month the Switchboard Collective wrote and adopted a manifesto, a party-line, or, if you are from that tradition, a confession of faith. Survival demanded it. Clear ideological unity was a necessity. In the course of signing the manifesto/covenant, some members were purged, like the long-haired veteran who could not take a stand against the war. The manifesto pledges to oppose the genocidal policies of our capitalist decadence, racism, sexism, elitism, cynicism and "laissez-faire do-your-own-thingism"; it pledges opposition to the Indochinese War, and supports their peoples' authentic struggle. It supports all struggles for self-determination, among people of color, poor whites, children, women, prisoners, and gay people. It pledges support to the radical Church, to hold frequent small group meetings, to engage in self-criticism, and to increase our work. Finally, it opposes the destruction of our sisters and brothers by drug use.[4]

In adopting this manifesto, the Switchboard became much more the Church. It abandoned the do-your-own-thing liberalism of that institution, which currently calls itself "church," and moved toward building itself into a radical counterinstitution to the state, identified with the poor and oppressed, demonstrating a life of service and intolerance for injustice.

Several of the clergy from local churches were upset not only by the language of the manifesto, but more, by what they called its "exclusivism," seen as inconsistent with the spirit of the Church. I will never understand how an Episcopal priest, whose collective demands confession of the creeds and episcopal confirmation, or a Baptist minister, whose collective requires believers' adult baptism, can find fault with what the Switchboard did. It took a stand and made a decision, when most churches are trying desperately to forget their own "manifesto," the gospel of Jesus.

*Youth and Spiritual Quest:* The murder of George Jackson, San Quentin, the SF Tac Squad, Attica, Santa Rita, junkies on the Avenue, a Freedom Meal at First Congo, a Switchboard phone number—what has all this to do with the spiritual quest of the young? Just everything!

Only two questions have to be answered here. Which youth are you talking about, and which spiritual quest? I am a partisan on both questions.

Movement youth, struggling with the demands of history and of the planet—peace, liberation, ecology—are the cutting edge, not only of their own generation but of the future. I choose them. Jesus freaks, various forms of navel-gazers, astrologers, Krishna chanters, Babaites, dope heads, and the liberal churches are escape artists we have all met before. They are all quests, to be sure, but the more important Quest is that one being made *toward* us by the power of history whose name we have known in the Scriptures, and whose name is now San Quentin, Attica, Santa Rita, Vietnam, junkie. In this quest God is doing a new thing. He is doing what lies beyond the power of any individual or group acting in history. He is raising up a new community, a Movement of people for peace and justice. Some of the Movement respond to this quest with God's name and some do not. But as there is one human race with one history, so there is one Power beyond history and one Movement for peace and justice.[5] Now is the day of our liberation. Seize the time!

1. George Jackson, *Soledad Brother* (New York: Bantam Books, 1970).

2. Weathermen Underground Communiqué, *The Berkeley Tribe*, September 3–9, 1971, p. 8.

3. Jackson, *op. cit.*

4. *Manifesto of the Berkeley Switchboard Collective*, August, 1971 (Free Church Publications, P.O. Box 9177, Berkeley, CA 94709).

5. Some of this wording from the "Ann Arbor Statement," August, 1971, Ann Arbor, Michigan, Clergy and Laymen Conference.

## Finding the People

I don't know what's wanted. I was "turned on" by my fellow participants who said, "We dig your rap—it's real heavy. Throw away the intellectual crap you wrote and 'tell it like it is!' "

What seemed clear to me at Block Island were two things: (1) the sincerity of the folks and (2) their need to tie into something concrete, real, relevant. I think they "dug" what I said because it is rooted in people. Do something! Or try, solve a problem, raise some "bread," respond to a crisis. But, I can't operate on crises alone. I need, once in a while, to spend "forty days in the desert" to think, to try to establish who I am, from whence I come, what it's all about. Why the misery? why the hurt? what in hell am I doing—*why?*

The Uptown Peoples–Northeastern Illinois University Center in the Uptown ghetto of Chicago: Native Americans, southern white migrants, Black Americans: hungry, tough, fucked up and fucked over, scuffling (literally) to survive. These *are* my people. We "make it together" (identify, communicate). We share a common past of grammar school "put-downs," high school failures, exploitative bosses, unannounced premeditated layoffs, sick mothers, bad-teeth brothers, pregnant sisters, and sibling-shared beds. Mrs. J. is forty-two and easily passes for fifty-five. Peggy Williams has a black eye and broken cheekbone from her alcoholic husband—happy birthday, Peg. Willie Brown's mother is dying of cancer at forty-two, and Betty Lester's sixteen-year-old daughter has run off and is missing now for over two weeks.

The "spiritual quest of youth" *should* be to follow jesus. Yes! my age and the amount of "dues" I've paid make it easy (at times) to be dogmatic. "Follow jesus" means all of the above—Mrs. J., Peggy Williams, Willie Brown, and Betty Lester. Or, fill in your own set of names. I see myself as a "primitive Christian," i.e., much of what the historical jesus said and did makes sense to me. It's the stuff that "came down" after Paul that I can't buy. No need to spell jesus with a supernatural capital letter. He was "together," don't you see, exactly because he wasn't "God." Just a "feeling dude" who did for others.

It seems to me that the youth of today (some of them) want to do. The difficulty is, "Do what?" Move to communes, become "Jesus freaks," "flower children," "Indians," "Black," "pot heads." No man! *do* who you are. Don't become an Indian because (1) you can't, (2) they won't let you, and (3) you are not.

The problem is twofold: (1) young people won't accept who they are or are not; and (2) without roots in person-oriented action they wallow around in abstract vagaries. Much of their wanderings are in themselves, indulgences in a personal ego trip. Lyrics to songs, no matter how true and creative, never put food in a poor person's mouth. The wearing of dirty, torn sixty-five-dollar suede jeans doesn't fool anyone—they only accurately describe your financial and mental condition. Rent money doesn't exist and your three-hundred-dollar stereo too loudly blares out who you really are. So the meanderings continue in the wrong valleys.

Just do, but do with your people in the North Shore communities, Westchester counties, and Cambridge ivy towers. Literally, knock on your neighbor's door and proclaim the "good news"—that we are racist, affluent, arro-

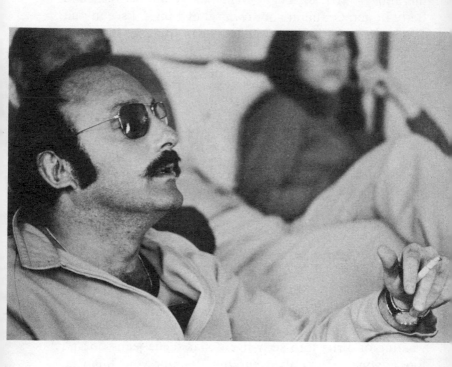

gant, hypercritical, and anti-Christ. Gather your neighbors and kin folk together and "turn them around," "pull their coattails," to "what's happening" and what needs to be done.

It seems overwhelmingly clear to me why Jesus never wrote. (He probably didn't know how.) He was too busy "out there" doing. The Last Supper may have been the first supper that his organization had time to consummate.

"Pay dues." Everybody pays dues. The problem is to pay your own dues because you can't pay mine. Nor can I pay yours. The workshop reinforced my feeling about this matter. I, once again, was made aware that while I can learn from you(th), empathize, sympathize, gain insights, I can't be you. My time, my dues were paid to a different union.

I'm not at all sure that what I'm doing is right, meaningful, and important; much less sure am I what is right, meaningful, and important for youth. However, I pragmatically resolve my dilemma by asking myself, "What is the alternative?" I cannot accept indecision or debilitating cynicism as a viable alternative. Given the choices of dealing with day-to-day problems and crises, or stagnating in no-action decision-making processes, it's "easy," i.e., imperative for me to act in favor of the former. I avoid the pitfall of attempting to generalize. The name of the game is involvement on an existential level—day to day—no more. Don't ask me to extrapolate from today's action to tomorrow, next week, or to a full-blown philosophy. The "dude" comes in off the streets because he's hurting. He needs help, almost always in the form of money, legal aid, advice, or just to talk. Now, "just to talk" is an interesting need because it flies in the face of the middle-class bureaucratic mind-set. "Time is money" and "a fool and his money soon part," and Euro-Western time is mechanical time; structured, organized, and divided into seconds, minutes, and hours. We don't have time to waste, but that "hurtin' cat" off the street has nothing but time. One dude put it succinctly in saying, "Time in jail and street time, it's all the same to me. We're all dying a little at a time anyhow, it's just a matter of when."

If you can "dig where he's coming from" it's easy to react—just stop what you're doing and "rap" with him— meet his need *now* and don't worry about time and schedules and deadlines because, "cheer up, one thing is for sure, tomorrow will be worse." It all fits in, it seems to me; Christ's admonition to "give the shirt off your back," the Berrigan brothers in Christian refuge, and Stringfellow's advice to a troubled minister who wondered where to continue to find money for a parishioner whom he suspected of drinking too much, and "whoring" too much, and neglecting herself too much. Stringfellow's suggestion to the minister was to sell the tapestries off the church wall and give the money to the woman. The good minister hung up: and we don't have time, and schedules have to be met, and we wonder why we don't know what to do.

WAYNE PROUDFOOT:

## The Search for Community

One manifestation of the current spiritual quest among the young seems to be a renewed search for community. This search has taken different forms. Literature and music arising from the youth culture may celebrate, for example, the intimacy involved in a small group sharing food or drugs, the anonymous community of a large gathering such as the Woodstock festival, or self-conscious attempts to create intimacy in the context of weekend sensitivity sessions or encounter groups. In each of these cases, the search is for immediate and tangible feelings of community. Each involves emphasis upon immediate sensory experience rather than upon a communal identity that is rooted in shared history and extends into a projected future.

The literature of the youth culture and of many of its apologists is filled with criticism of the loss of opportunities for the experience of intimacy and the depersonalization of contemporary technological society. Such a society is charged with encouraging a competitive atmosphere in which individuals are rewarded for treating others as pawns in their own struggles for success. Against this depersonalized society is juxtaposed a vision of a new form of community in which immediate sensory experience and enjoyment of personal relations are once again given priority.

What kind of community is being sought? Churches have always been communities of persons and have often interpreted one of their central tasks as the proclamation and representation of what human community might become. It might be instructive, then, for the church to attend to this new search for community and to the resources which it might bring to its encounter with the spiritual quest of the young.

In the first part of this paper the underlying model of community which informs the recent liberal tradition will be sketched, especially with regard to the understanding of governance, and of the importance of language and temporality in human experience. The same issues will then be examined in connection with the alternative vision reflected in some elements of the youth culture. Some possible reasons for the espousal of this new vision will be suggested. Finally possible responses of the church to this new search will be considered.

The tradition of political liberalism has been criticized from several quarters for its lack of an adequate understanding of community.[1] Liberal notions of freedom, of justice, and of governance are based on the concept of the autonomy and sovereignty of the individual as articulated in the Enlightenment. The individual is sovereign. His will is his own and he relates to other individuals as a free agent. He may enter into conflict or into contracts, but he is never defined by these engagements.

The interpretation of political community which is appropriate to this tradition is provided by the theory of the social contract. An individual voluntarily surrenders certain freedoms in return for the right to expect similar behavior from others. A contract between individuals in a state to obey civil laws and to provide sanctions against persons who disobey yields a minimum amount of order which may actually increase the freedom of each individual. If all agree not to murder, then the individual citizen need not constantly beware. If laws are created which sanction respect for private property, it is not incumbent upon each citizen to protect his own holdings singlehand-edly. There is nothing inherent in the laws which demands that they be obeyed. They do not reflect any absolute or cosmic order. They are founded only in the contractual agreement between individuals. The individual may enter a contract or leave it. There is nothing in the contract which enters into his self-definition. Each individual is au-tonomous and is independent of any contract which he might choose to enter.

In this view the establishment of community is under-stood to serve the individual and to increase his freedom. But there was another widespread interpretation of a community of individuals in eighteenth-century liberal thought, particularly in economic theory. Community was held to be a natural outcome of the independent and com-petitive actions of productive individuals. Each person was encouraged to develop himself to the fullest and to realize his own potentialities. The aggregate then was believed to be a community. This definition of community as a collec-tion of individuals each pursuing his own ends demanded a certain faith in the harmony of the aggregate. Adam Smith employed the phrase "the invisible hand of God" to describe the ordering principle that would mold a commu-nity out of the competitive marketplace. Faith in such a principle became the basis for the laissez-faire doctrine in economic and political theory. If each individual worked for his own personal ends and did not directly infringe upon the freedom of others, competition would ensure the survival of the fittest and the building of a stronger group or nation. Weber's description of the economic efficacy of the Calvinist notion of individual salvation suggests one source of motivation in accord with this individualism.

Liberalism in political and economic theory is consistent with the empiricist spirit. It is not accidental that Locke, the author whose theory of the social contract is reflected in the Declaration of Independence, also developed an epistemology whereby knowledge is understood to consist of the impressions made upon the senses by events and objects in the external world, and of relations between these events. Words are held to be meaningful when they can be tied down to direct sensory experience. Experimentation proceeds by the forming of hypotheses and the empirical testing of these hypotheses. Such experimentation has a public validity. Words are not primarily expressions for private or subjective experience. The adjudication of disputed claims involves the search for what is actually the case. The claim of the private individual is subjected to public scrutiny. Words are seen to be rooted in the experience of a common world. Arguments can be made and truth can be sought by verifying or contradicting specific hypotheses. Words are also means by which private individuals enter into public contracts. Words are the primary means for rational communication between persons and for the establishment of public conventions and laws.

Time is understood by the liberal tradition as the arena in which goals are pursued and achieved. The attention of an individual is directed toward the past from which he came and toward the future for which he is laying plans. His own identity is rooted in the past and projected toward the future. History is the arena of progress. Attention is deployed toward the past and the future in order to orient activity in the present. Memory thus plays a critical role in the identity of the self, as does anticipation. Planning for the future often involves the delay of immediate gratification in favor of long-range goals which also contribute to the present identity of the self.

During the nineteenth and early twentieth centuries, this liberal understanding of the sovereignty of the individual, the autonomous ego confronting a field of alternatives and possibilities and competing with other selves in the open marketplace, was instrumental in the development of modern society. The adventurer, the business entrepreneur of the Industrial Revolution, the inventor, the hero who opened new frontiers in the wilderness terrain of America or in the life of the mind was the model for all men. Competition was encouraged, and it facilitated the development of skills which might otherwise have lain dormant. There were new worlds to conquer. Frederick Jackson Turner's hypothesis concerning the influence of the frontier on the American spirit provides a helpful interpretation of this period.

Members of the current generation of youth find themselves in a country and a world where there are few frontiers left. We have long since reached the Pacific, and suburban shopping centers have sprung up everywhere. In the nineteenth century the adventurer hero could be and often was uncomfortable in conventional society. If he had trouble accommodating to the demands of intimacy and family life, he could throw his gun over his shoulder and head west to do battle with the Indians or to claim a homestead or search for gold. A few years later a more enterprising and perhaps more educated personality could build a railroad empire, invest his time and energy in developing a business, and still remain relatively free of the demands and pressures created by the intimacy of family life and personal relations. The lone adventurer, the business entrepreneur, the inventor in his laboratory, the scholar have long been models of individual achievement in the American cultural context. Persons who are now in elementary or high schools face a world in which that frontier has finally been exhausted. After the Pacific was reached the United States fought several wars, the motives of which were mixed between an economic interest to expand our sphere of influence and thus our markets and an evangelical interest in spreading the democratic form of government. Now even that extension of our moral frontier, which carried us several decades beyond the settling of the Pacific coast, has come up against limits. The infinitely expanding markets that are necessary for the continual expansion on which capitalism is based are no longer available. The crowding of the population of the earth, the scarcity of natural resources, the increasing awareness that the environment of the planet is not an infinitely extended frontier, but is, for the purposes of living, a closed box that is being polluted in such a way as to close us in even more tightly—all of these are aspects of a kind of closure which is keenly felt by young people today.

More important than this scarcity of physical resources is the scarcity of channels for meaningful and productive labor. A few years ago a person leaving high school had several conventional alternatives which would allow him or her to leave home and to enter existing institutions that would afford some meaning in themselves and within which he or she could build an identity apart from that provided by the family. The armed services, an occupation, marriage, and the university provided such institutions. Each of these, in differing ways, may now seem to a high school graduate to offer less certain meaning than it did in the past. The armed services once offered an opportunity to defend the country or to fight for liberty around the world. Enlistment was seen as an opportunity for service in a noble cause and provided one route by which many boys escaped the parochialism of their home environments and moved out into a wider world. The armed services have now become discredited among many because of the campaigns in which this country has been and is engaged. For many they no longer provide an honorable pursuit at a time in which an individual is seeking to forge his own identity. Morale is low in the armed services, and there is widespread resistance to the Southeast Asian war.

Jobs are more difficult to find than they have been during the last few decades. It is increasingly difficult for high school dropouts or returning veterans to find work. The depletion of world markets for American materials and the transition from a wartime to a peacetime economy will probably exacerbate this condition in the near future.

Marriage no longer provides the sense of security that once seemed to accompany it. In the past marriage served as the rite by which one entered into adulthood sexually and took on new responsibilities as the head of a household. Greater opportunities for sexual experimentation and maturation outside of marriage and the increasing difficulty of finding work have detracted from the efficacy of marriage as a meaning-giving institution. While it is certainly true that it is still possible to find meaning and to grow in marriage, the institution of marriage alone no longer carries the meaning that it once did.

At one time it could be assumed that parents who managed to save enough money in order to enroll their son or daughter in college had guaranteed that person success in the world. Entrance to college and eventual graduation was assurance of a meaningful and relatively lucrative job. The professions, the business world, and related sectors of the economy needed more college-trained personnel than the universities could provide. Possession of a college degree was a guarantee of job security. For others the attainment of a graduate degree provided an opportunity to contribute meaningfully to a particular field of knowledge. Now the attainment of a college degree provides no guarantee of job security. Many graduates have been unable to find appropriate employment. And it is becoming increasingly clear to students at all levels that they are being prepared for a society which has no need for their skills. The number of doctorates in many fields is rapidly overtaking and exceeding the demand, so that even the achievement of the Ph.D. does not ensure a meaningful and productive vocation. At a time when some are speaking of a "post-scarcity economy" and when futurologists predict that there may soon be enough consumer goods to satisfy all and to eliminate poverty throughout the world, the scarcity of land, of open space, of meaningful and productive labor, and of frontiers of all kinds is constricting the world in which we live.

1. Philip Slater, *The Pursuit of Loneliness: American Culture at the Breaking Point* (Boston: Beacon Press, 1970); R. Jackson Wilson, *In Quest of Community: Social Philosophy in the United States, 1860–1920* (London: Oxford University Press, 1968); and Robert Paul Wolff, *The Poverty of Liberalism* (Boston: Beacon Press, 1968).

## Jack, the Fabulous Beanstalk, and the Magic Harp

Another perspective on the quest of the young is afforded by the story of Jack and the Beanstalk. Jack makes three journeys up and down the beanstalk. On the first two trips he captures a basket of golden eggs and the magic hen who lays the golden eggs. Thus Jack would seem to have provided not only sufficiently but superlatively for the financial security of both his mother and himself. He elects nevertheless to make a third and final journey to that other world. Why would he do this? What more can he gain? He has everything necessary for his worldly security. Freud, in commenting upon this, is reported to have said, "Of course Jack returned a third time! Money does not represent an infantile wish-fulfillment." That is, in terms of our story, we are confronted with individuals and nations with vast quantities of wealth but who experience poverty in their inmost being. So Jack makes his third journey, hears the music of the magic harp, steals it away, is pursued by the giant, fells the stalk, thereby slaying the giant, possesses the harp and its mysteriously satisfying music, and lives happily ever after. While the financial security represented by the golden eggs is a necessary precondition of the third journey, this security becomes meaningful by virtue of the transcending music which is truly satisfying.

The story is reminiscent of the description of the four aims of life in Hinduism. The first three are *kama* (pleasure), *artha* (power and success), and *dharma* (responsible and dutiful moral action). The complete human life requires appropriate fulfillment of each of these three aims.

A life lacking in any of these three aims is fragmented and distorted. On the other hand, however, if only these three aims are met, then the life of the person remains incomplete. The underlying assumption seems to be this: the bodily requirement for pleasure and the social requirement for self-sufficiency (power and success) and responsible behavior do not exhaust the potentialities of human life. The life of the person seeks more than gratification of sensual-sociological desires and demands. Hence a fourth aim is included as necessary for the completion of life: namely, *moksa* (liberation). Liberation here is to be understood as a transcending of the other three aims so as to enable the individual to realize his true self-being. Furthermore, this spiritual-psychological necessity is undergirded by a social support system in which the possibility is provided for the individual (either by himself or with his wife) to leave the social structures and enter, as a forest-dweller, a period of meditation upon the true meaning of life. Without this, the true potentiality of life remains unrealized, the person is not completed.

May we not, then, look upon Jack's quest for the beautiful music of the magic harp as a dynamic of completion which transcends the ordinary requirements of dutiful responsibility on behalf of the demands for worldly security? Then, by the same token—though at the risk of stating the obvious—may we not see the spiritual quest of the young as an attempt to incorporate, both individually and societally, the insight that the completion of life requires going beyond the ordinary requirements sanctioned by the established orders?

# III

## Confronting the "Sacred Yes"

Arriving at dawn in a still and brilliant light,
I sat among new-made peaks,
Savoring the salt fresh taste
Of the pristine snow on sand and slag,
Abandoned mines and bulldozed mountain scars,
With my feet on the festive roof of the world,
Nothing to feel but joy,
Nowhere to go but down.

*"Climbing Mount Bross, August 1970,"*
*by Joan Webber*

JAMES FOREST:

## The Generation-Not-Buying-It Today

The number of persons who can understand wholeheartedly St. Paul's statement, "They call us dead people—but it is we who are alive," are still few, despite there being a thousand dropouts today for every one or two ten years ago. Even for those few, the voluntary poverty which is so prominent a part of their life-style, one of their garments of freedom, is often only an episode in their lives rather than the source of their continuing liberation.

The trappings of an alternative life-style are far more in evidence than the essence they originally clothed. It is easy to listen to the Rolling Stones singing about life "just a breath away," and death "just a shot away," without mulling over the war in Southeast Asia or the coffin-spaces rented to slum families in wealthy America. The president says, "Power to the people." Admen headline, "Right on." Co-option, it has been called—and the technique is at least as old as Constantine's absorption of Christianity; or rather, to note Dick Gregory's distinction—Constantine's establishment of Churchianity.

No more on St. Mark's Place than on Wall Street is the promised land in evidence. There may have been a population explosion in the counter-culture, but the maturation process has been less hurried.

Certainly drugs have been a factor in that, seeming to alternate between blessing and curse. On the one hand, experiences with LSD and similar chemicals that dissolved barricades between consciousness and subconsciousness resulted for many in a flooding sense of the miraculous, a discovery of unimagined possibilities for communion, an end to every kind of alienation and inner solitude. We could be astonished with the mere presence of someone else—to feel, even at a distance, the furnace warmth pouring from another's life. We could perceive the auras that surround and describe another. We could play back and reexperience evolution, the succession of epochs, the constant turn-taking of life and death. We could understand the efforts of theologians and mystics to describe eternity as a state in which the experience of time was no longer equivalent to solitary confinement. The steep, surrounding wall of "I" was no longer impassable.

On the other hand, we were slow in realizing that the drug experience was largely dependent on what one brought to it. Those drawn to LSD originally, when Leary was still at Harvard, tended to have a well-defined interest in what some have called the inner life; there were at least some of the rudiments of religious awareness, some sense of an Essence that is holy, holding, centering, warm; something caring; something that we catch flickers of in every experience of love or joy.

But for those in whom fear had replaced conscience as the mainspring in life, drug experiences—while breaking the monotony—were too often like sky-diving experiences in which the parachute never opened.

One saw more intensely on chemicals only what had been sensed before—for those who had sensed God, there was a chance of "seeing" God; for those who had sensed nothingness and meaninglessness, it was the vacuum that was amplified.

The deterioration of the drug-centered segments of the counter-culture finally provoked a realization of the huge irony it is that we critics of technology had become the advocates of its final assault: the technologizing and manipulation of consciousness itself; we anticonsumers found ourselves pushing the ultimate commodity, New Improved God Experience, with a small-type notice on the back stating that a demon might have to substitute at the last moment.

Early optimism with electoral politics seems to have gone a similar course, enthusiastic hope finally colliding with the reinforced concrete of the Democratic Party in Chicago in 1968. The real event in that auditorium was the burning, not of draft records, but of the ballots that had been cast in the primaries and of the reports of public preferences from opinion-survey corporations. In both parties, housebroken candidates were nominated.

But it was a real schooling, of a sort that almost never occurs in classrooms. Some unfiltered contact with reality was made. It helped us begin realizing that, in terms of our economy, we are regarded as rentable objects, valuable insofar as we produce profits. Rentable objects, pure and simple; that and nothing more. Unless one is to note the other side of the coin, on which we are pictured as garbage-disposal units. For it is necessary that we be addicted to the consequences of those processes into which we are rented. Keeping up with consumption demands is not to be poor. Poverty is measured according to our inability to consume on schedule.

We realized, in terms of the military, something even more devastating: we are not only rentable objects disposing of purchasable services with our reward for being rented, but we are ourselves disposable objects.

And we realized that even the churches had their part, a crucial role in fact: assuring us that our armies, schools, supermarkets, family, and work roles, that our standard of living has the approval of *the* Highest Authority. ("Oh, a little virtuous tinkering wouldn't hurt, certainly things could be improved here and there, an occasional Harlem or My Lai omitted. But these must be recognized as tragic exceptions, not things to prompt expansive doubts. Emphasize those things and you're playing into the hands of the God-hating communists! God forbid!")

The worms had long ago invaded the apple: Constantine in the church, Custer in America, a succession of immaculate presidents and generals in Vietnam. Still it is a shock finding nothing left in otherwise shiny apple skins.

So there has been cynicism—among the young nearly as much as among the old. After all, our life-style, our music, our clothes, our hair—the marketing has come quickly. Nor has the burning of humans become less frequent for the raising of placards in front of the White House. Recession does not yet apply to the perimeter of slums. The comic bitterness of Abbie Hoffman's *Steal This Book* probably makes more sense than Alicia Bay Laurel's *Living on the Earth* to kids who either can't find a route back to the land or find urban and military realities require delaying any rural exodus.

Remarkably, the cynicism, though eminently justified, is still not dominant; one is forced to wonder whether the weed of hope flourishes best where the soil is most stingy. For the hope is flourishing, and the soil it thrives in couldn't be much stingier: Hiroshima and Dresden seem to have been taking continuous encores for a quarter century.

I explain the hope religiously. "They call us dead people, but it is we who are alive." To live where life is officially declared impossible, to hope when it is fair to call a small nation the Land of Burning Children—I find no vocabulary to use but a religious one.

It is certainly the religious element that runs through

those few who have caused others to feel their pulse again. I've heard it said that it is a joy to hear Rosa Parks singing in church. I can stand witness myself to the contagious ecstasy of Allen Ginsberg's poem prayings, his mantra songs from Blake, even his charming of vandals and—more difficult—hostile columnists with chant and poetry and laughter; after that, belief in the tumbling walls of Jericho comes easy. And I stand witness to Dorothy Day, first remembering her in prayer, calm, centered, as if carved from wood, a stubborn peace about her. Or Thomas Merton, in his monk's robes, laughing on the floor, holding his belly, overcome with joy at the Catholic Worker smells we hitchhikers had brought within our shoes in a three-day hitch to that antiseptic monastery. Or Dan Berrigan, or Kerouac, or Solzhenitsyn, or Tolkien, or Levertov, or Bly, or King, or Malcolm X . . . religious currents running through each of them, and most often well advertised, at the surface; a boast; a brag.

It isn't a religiousness that is institutionally captive. Roman Catholic that I am, I admit delight that so much of it comes from my quarter. But neither Ginsberg nor Rosa Parks nor Art Waskow claim to be Roman Catholic. And some of them claim no particular tradition at all—perhaps, vaguely, they claim the Unified Buddhist Quaker Hasidic Zen Catholic and Miscellaneous Church. The traditional and orthodox, the playful and mischievous heretics—all prancing around the same bonfire, the same blaze of state-approved idols; and all aware of the mystery we surround, our Harpo Marx standing in the sight of the universe, the importance of celebrating life, the necessity of recycling the mud and straw (and the plastic and aluminum) gods that the rulers of church and state keep manufacturing.

The religious dimension—the one place to live where life isn't a duty. A dimension of consciousness that doesn't confuse habitability with ease of entrance—a consciousness that immediately prefers mountain ranges to low doorsills.

A dimension of relief—the liberating acceptance of what everyone occasionally intuits but hardly ever dares believe: that there is a center, that God isn't a wallpaper word covering nothingness, that it is possible to climb out of our fears and even out of our graves.

There is something contagious about it. Some are glimpsing that religious life, in its various forms, in the midst of its ironic disguise of voluntary poverty, is the most evolved form of hedonism. It answers the question, "How can I be happy?" And it does so when the alternative proposals—of five-year plans and house payments and omnivorous solemnity and conveyor-belt vacations—have led to the edge of extinction.

At that fire in Milwaukee—the one where we recycled all those draft files—as soon as the flame was struck, one of the felons started singing, "Ding dong, the witch is dead, the wicked witch is dead!" He danced for joy. And we laughed and held each other while waiting for the police to come.

## The Tradition of the Spiritual Life

It is sad to find the young limited to a vulgar contemporaneity. Perhaps their immediate elders are partly to blame for this limitation. Reading a recent theological book like *Soundings* (1962), a symposium of modern-minded Anglican clergy, I am shocked to find scarcely a philosophical or theological work cited published more than a decade before the date of the book—and nothing before Barth, Bultmann, and Bonhoeffer. One could find some plausibility to this contemporaneity were one in the world of the physical or even the social sciences; but, in the humanities and even more in religion there are truths which do not change from generation to generation, or from century to century. With relief, I turn to Dom Hubert von Zeller's *Approach to Monasticism* (1960) and discover that St. Benedict and St. Bernard are referred to with as much respect as Thomas Merton, the recently deceased admirable American Cistercian, or to Père Louis Bouyer's *Introduction to Spirituality* (1961), in which all the classical names of Eastern as well as Western ascetic and mystic thought are seriously cited.

When genuine young idealists rejoin the human race, they will find the traditional alternative paths or ways open to them. They can live "in the world, but not of it." And that is the way for most men. But that, the modern and Protestant and secular answer, is not the only one. The Catholic Church, Catholic Christendom, offers as rich and varied a series of life-styles as can be found. It is full of ways and of models for secular or quasi-secular imitation. Think of the religious who work as Christian Brothers, of the nuns who work in hospitals, of the friars—the

Franciscans, the Dominicans and the Cistercians (or Trappists)—these out of Western Christendom. Then think of the monks of the Eastern church, who follow, at Mount Athos and at Mount Sinai and elsewhere, the Rule of St. Basil. Think of those who live in monasteries and "would have an abbot rule them"; and then of the more primitive types, those who live the idiorhythmic life of the *skete*, the tiny community gathered around their spiritual father, and, finally, the hermits (traditionally, in the East, the most spiritually advanced). Another William James might write a humanistic *Varieties of Monastic Experience*.

Jacob Needleman, a young professor of philosophy at San Francisco State College who has studied the "new religions" (chiefly Indian, Japanese, and Tibetan) of the California young, and who has wisely meditated on his observations of these cults, has this to say: "it is an indication of our twentieth-century American idea of religion that monasticism is by and large considered on the fringe, as secondary to church religion. Of course, this is a complete reversal of the historical relationship between Church and monastery, where the latter was the source of the life of the former."

The monasteries are at the present moment having their difficulties in recruiting novices; but one Benedictine has recently—I think with justice—prophesied that within the next twenty years many of the hippies will be knocking for admission to the monasteries. Only, adds the same Benedictine, the monasteries "better be genuine"—not relaxed, or modernized, or adapted, or otherwise made easy.

The lack of instruction in the spiritual life and methods for attaining it is a shortcoming of the Christian Church as it exists today. Like Dom Aelred Graham, Mr. Needleman finds the Church failing the spiritually minded young by not giving them, as the Zen Buddhists do, or as Vedanta does, systematic training in meditation and prayer—even in physical posture as a preparatory spiritual discipline. He remarks upon the "absence in [our contemporary religious forms] of practical technique, method, and discipline. Various rituals, prayers, services, and the like, no longer function as a part of the mechanics of the religious process, but mainly as an emotional lift. . . ." They "help to preserve the quality of life we lead rather than transform it." The young have "heard exhortations, commandments, prescriptions by the basketful, but nobody was telling them how to be able to follow them."

Suppose a physician read aloud, or the patients read to each other, some accurate medical textbook. Would it relieve the suffering, however eloquently read? The analogue is Needleman's. I amplify: Is not actual treatment necessary for a cure? Reading Freud or Fromm or Horney or Stack Sullivan will not take the place of "analysis"; it may even make the patient worse. The suggestion behind the analogy seems to be that sin is disease—is, as the Buddhists say, ignorance, desire, and suffering. Most of us have heard in our modern churches few theoretical sermons on sin or salvation, few reasoned theological discourses, the equivalents perhaps of textbooks; but we have heard perhaps even yet fewer instructions on the methods of spirituality. Possibly the Sunday sermon is not the place for more than exhortation; but, if so, and even if not, there should be some regular weekday services like the old-fashioned Methodist "class-meetings" and the longer-surviving midweek prayer meetings. Already, Roman Catholics are adding gatherings for extempore Pentecostal prayer to the liturgical prayer of the church. But I do not think prayer and meditation can reach their heights without instruction.

"Lord, teach us how to pray." It is hard to think that our Lord did not do more than offer a model form of words.

If the young spiritual questers are to learn how to meditate and engage in *mental* prayer, they must certainly have their teachers. Are our clergy—our parish priests and our chaplains of students—equipped and ready to teach these spiritual disciples?

Spiritual disciplines, spiritual exercises—these are what the young want, and what the old ought never to have ceased practicing; yet somehow, under the influence of yesteryear's modernism, they have dropped out. Years ago I read a book an Indian prince published, chiefly for his own people, though he wrote in a kind of English. His book was a manual of Yoga exercises, illustrated by photographs of the venerable prince in the various postures. What I have not forgotten is his express rubric that these exercises must be done facing some god-symbol—an image or a crucifix; and "if you have no god, draw an orange, sun-like circle and affix it to the wall in front of you." This mode of combining physical exercise with spiritual orientation is missing from the Western world.

But the Christian Church, especially but by no means exclusively in the monastic tradition, has preserved many ancient disciplines and exercises. There is the rule of silence: not to speak unless one could as willingly keep silence; the silent meal; the silent meeting for worship. (We live in a world full of media-noises and others—of jukeboxes and piped-in music, a world uncomfortable without "background," unlistened to but terrifying by its absence.) There is the practice of solitude, permanent or periodic— the "going apart for a while," the Retreat, the temporary withdrawal from "the daily round, the common task."

There is the discipline of fasting, which can be assumed

for the purpose not of enhanced comeliness but of "bringing the body under." The seven deadly sins include an American favorite—greed, gluttony, the perpetual snack, the insatiate mouth.

Fénelon salutarily reminds intellectuals, old and young, that "the mind must fast also as well as the body." A good discipline for Lent or any other season would be an abstinence from newspaper and magazine reading. The eyes have their greed as well as the mouth. And most professional readers know the greed of "covering ground," of "keeping up," and need to remember the practice of philosophers like Benjamin Whichcote, whose modest boast it was that he read *non multa sed multum,* not many but much.

In his early lectures, Emerson has much to say of spiritual hygiene as he outlines the Way for his "scholar," his spiritually questing young man; and he commonly makes some embarrassed remarks about the utility to the "scholar" of manual labor. Of its use to the monk, St. Benedict speaks in his Rule. Adventurous it need not be, still less should it be exhausting, for its value is therapeutic and disciplinary: splitting wood, weeding a garden, raking hay: I limit myself to elementary examples. Let me add, under manual labor, the habit of walking. Those who don't own a motorcar need not hitchhike for rides in the cars of others.

Traditionally, spiritual exercises belong to the ascetic stage or period of the spiritual life, the preparation for mystical experience, the direct experience of God. The disciplines aim at a settled state of recollection, union with the "unconditioned," a state of peace and joy. The use of drugs is an attempted shortcut to such supreme states of serenity and ecstasy as mystical theology postulates. There

are no shortcuts to the mountains; as Hawthorne reminded us, there is no "celestial railroad." Such "new religions" as promise wisdom, recollection, and ecstasy in ten
easy lessons are new versions of old heresies and frauds.

Having spoken this much of the spiritual quests of the
young as, at their best, a resurgence of primal and permanent quests of man, as current examples of man's hunger
and thirst for real righteousness, for the infinite love and
wisdom, I want to end with some words on a persistent,
but today critical, problem, that of the relation of religion
to culture. Long ago, reading the nineteenth-century sages
Newman and Arnold, I formulated to myself: Newman
subsumes culture under religion, while Arnold reverses the
subsumption. This is an intellectual maneuver I cannot
emulate. Religion (high or low) is clearly the more fundamental; yet I cannot but see in culture a necessary balance
or check on religion. Religion can better get on without
culture than culture without religion. To be sure, without
religion, culture can become, if it is the culture of the gen-
tleman, superficiality, urbanity, smooth manners, amateur-
ism; if it is the culture of the professors, mere "booklearn-
ing," erudition, intelligence without commitment or moral
responsibility, connoisseurship, skepticism. But without
culture, religion can be superstition, fanaticism, bigotry,
intolerance, and obscurantism. Religion stands in need simultaneously of some restraint by culture and of some relief from it. Arnold's "Hebraism and Hellenism," in his
*Culture and Anarchy*, is too patronizing of both the Anglican establishment and the bibliolatric nonconformists, but
it can serve as partial text. In a Shelburne essay, "Criticism," Paul Elmer More finds in Erasmus and Sainte-

Beuve (and I might add Montaigne) sound checks on the influence of St. Paul and Luther. Christian humanism is the combination of religion and culture, of learning and spirituality. This proper balance—I better say—is ideal, difficult, and precarious.

There is indeed great religious thirst and appetite among today's young, even though much of it is naturally crude and elementary; but I am disturbed and disquieted by the evidences of anti-intellectualism which accompany it, the more disturbing since Americans are endemically anti-intellectual. In our universities, there is a demand only for what is judged "relevant" by the unread and inexperienced. The desire for the "existential" (at its crudest a synonym for "relevant") rules out the patient acquisition of knowledge, either as an end in itself (for the most part, at the least a harmless form of contemplation, a form of scholarly busy-work) or as material for philosophical shaping. If, two or three generations ago, the German type of research-scholarship seemed in need of subordination to a more critically oriented type, now a responsible criticism itself is suspect. It is granted that "exact sciences" cannot be learned by a free-for-all discussion; but I can indeed wonder whether, in the world of the humanities or of spirituality, one man's opinion is as good as another. It is "undemocratic" to say so, but the principle of hierarchy is at least as important as the principle of equality. All men—and all values—are not, except in specified ways, equal. There is indeed a "diversity of gifts"; but there is also what the Renaissance called the principle of "degree."

It is easy to confound *a* culture with culture, *a* civilization with civilization, though we must not forget that even a civilization in decay still preserves some of its virtue. But let not the young, let not any of us, in objecting to a culture deemed obsolete, fail to build the counter-, or future-, culture with the full knowledge of the values of our own traditional culture, including our traditional religion.

## Shaman Sunday

As a child I sometimes imagined that the family whose name I carried was not my real family, that I had been adopted and not told, and someday I would meet my true family and mysteriously recognize those brothers and sisters from whom I had long been separated. Until then, I would carry my solitude with me like an invisible prayer rug.

Though people of all ages have carried that burden, young people now seem to feel it most keenly. Many are leaving the families into which they were born and moving into communes with the families they have chosen. In doing so, they have tried to shake off a culture which will be remembered chiefly for the efficiency of its weapons and for its wealth of knowledge on how to kill. The house built on death will not stand, and whoever is born there must, like the hermit crab, go in search of another if he is to survive.

This search leads many young people to those cultures where the spirit is stronger than the machine. I do not think a disillusioned Christian can put on the culture of an American Indian, or a Jew, or a Buddhist, however attractive the faith, and expect to be comfortable. Nor should he have to go elsewhere for what Christianity can give him: "I am the resurrection, and the life: he that believeth in me, though he were dead, yet shall he live: And whosoever liveth and believeth in me shall never die" (St. John 11: 25–26).

The Church is a family which includes both the living and the dead, for the lives of its saints are present, not past, and the man of faith is he who can raise the dead as well as heal the living. We know, of course, of the more spectacular instances of this: Lazarus comes forth in his shroud and Jairus' daughter returns from death to her family at Jesus' command.

But there is another kind of death not always named as such: the paralysis of the spirit through fear, hatred, anxiety, madness, or whatever state of soul keeps a man in bondage. When it is accompanied by wealth or power, it is often mistakenly called life. When it is accompanied by insight, it is called the road to freedom, or losing your life in order to save it. Rilke describes this experience so well that I can do no better than to quote him here:

A person removed from his own room, almost without preparation and transition, and set upon the height of a great mountain range, would feel . . . an unparalleled insecurity, an abandonment to something inexpressible would almost annihilate him. He would think himself falling or hurled out into space, or exploded into a thousand pieces: what a monstrous lie his brain would have to invent to catch up with and explain the state of his senses! . . . That mankind has in this sense been cowardly has done life endless harm; the experiences that are called "visions," the whole so-called "spirit-world," death, all those things that are so closely akin to us, have by daily parrying been so crowded out of life that the senses with which we could have grasped them are atrophied. To say nothing of God.[1]

The Church can make the new space friendly to us by reminding us that not all residences have windows and walls. Through the liturgy, it brings us together at a place where our differences do not matter, and it gives us the shared experience of a power that is not of this world.

"Ritual is mythology made alive," writes Campbell in *The Masks of God*, "and its effect is to convert men into angels." [2] Is this asking too much? I don't think so.

Among many "primitive" people, the religious leader is the shaman. As priest, he receives the dances and chants— the liturgy—in visions sent to him by the gods for the spiritual health of the tribe. As healer, he sends his own soul to fetch the soul of a dying man from the land of the dead. He knows the way because he has been there himself. A Tungus shaman shows the coming of his power in these words:

Before I commenced to shamanize, I lay sick for a whole year. . . . After that, my ancestors began to shamanize with me. They stood me up like a block of wood and shot at me with their bows until I lost consciousness. They cut up my flesh, separated my bones, counted them, and ate my flesh raw. . . .

The same thing happens to every Tungus shaman. Only after his shaman ancestors have cut up his body in this way and separated his bones can he begin to practice. [3]

He is, in a sense, crucified to rise again.

The passion and resurrection of Christ belong to history and to God. Shouldn't the church have a service, as the shaman does, to show this experience of dying and returning on a personal level? For we die to each other daily in a thousand ways, and only you can bring your brother back to life again, through compassion and sacrifice. Let such a service show that family ties are stronger than death when you have found your true family, the family of man in the likeness of the living God.

## The Lesson from the Service for Shaman Sunday

*Readers:* Man, Woman, Child, Death.

MAN: The voice said, Cry. And he said, What shall I cry? All flesh is grass, and all the goodliness thereof is as the flower of the field: The grass withereth, the flower fadeth: because the spirit of the Lord bloweth upon it: surely the people is grass.

WOMAN: The grass withereth, the flower fadeth: but the word of our God shall stand forever.[4]

MAN: When she awoke, she stood among deer,
felt a deer's features masking her face,
and far ahead, Death walked in his woods.

WOMAN: "Lord Death, Lord Death, give me my face.
Let me return to tuck in my child
who won't fall asleep if nobody rocks him."

MAN: Death baited his traps and settled his snares,
twisted his spittle and held up a thread,
wove her a collar and knotted it fast.

DEATH:   *"You may go this one night."*

MAN: She flew past a thousand towns to her own.
No light shone in her baby's room,
no light shone at the father's window.

Throwing her deerskin aside, she leaped
and stood by the father rocking his son.
All night they rocked, the three together,

and when she returned, she stood among foxes.

WOMAN:     "Lord Death, Lord Death, give me a road.
           My child is restless if I don't rock him."

MAN:       He checked the thread that furrowed her neck,
           lowered his nets and baited his snares,
           showed her again the way to the world.

DEATH:                  *"You may go this one night."*

MAN:       Half the night she fled over mountains,
           cities that welcomed and soldiers that burned,
           leaping the twilight streets to her own.

           And wrapping her child in the skin of the fox,
           she sang him a nightsong of thickets and owls,
           the lovesongs of foxes and deer to his father.

           And when she returned, she stood among lions.

WOMAN:     "Lord Death! Lord Death! Give me my life.
           Let me return to my love and my child."

MAN:       Death took his spittle and mended the collar.

DEATH:     "Unless you can snap the thread in my hand,
           you may go this night and never again."

MAN:       Morning broke on the seven seas,
           lighting the trees as she sprang over stars.
           She wrapped the child in her lion's skin,
           and cried to the father,

WOMAN:                          "Fasten this thread
           Death winds my life on a spool of fear."

MAN:       Already they saw it seeking the dark.

           The father caught it.

           It turned to a knife that whittled his hand,
           his hand was harder and turned it to blood.

It twisted and kindled a river of fire,
it spread like an ocean and rose like a flood.

He gave his arm for a sliver of land
where one would perish but three might stand,
and grass grew up between them and the place
where the child's mother had lost her face.

And when they returned, they stood among
men
and walked with joy in the world's weather,
and even their shadows shouted together.

WOMAN:    I am the door: by me if any man enter in, he
shall be saved, and shall go in and out, and find
pasture. The thief cometh not, but for to steal,
and to kill, and to destroy: I am come that they
might have life, and that they might have it
more abundantly.

MAN:    I am the good shepherd: the good shepherd giv-
eth his life for the sheep. . . . My sheep hear my
voice, and I know them, and they follow me:
And I give unto them eternal life; and they
shall never perish, neither shall any man pluck
them out of my hand. My Father, which gave
them me, is greater than all; and no man is able
to pluck them out of my Father's hand.[5]

WOMAN:    My son was born during the Great War.
Every morning he rattles his crib
and babbles alone to invisible teachers.

CHILD:             "Mother, mother,
you play the piano, announcing my flight.
My first step leads to the moon and the sun,
my next to the serpent whose skin is darkness,

my third to the angels and clowns, my brothers
I lost when I stumbled and woke in this world."

WOMAN:    My son was born during the Great War.
Every day we write to his father.
Every day the conscriptor appears
and Death follows, dragging a sack.
I play the piano, my child dances,
and Death gathers the day's slaughter
and sees that my child is very beautiful,
softer than milkweed, ready to fly.

Crying, my child taught me to listen.
Every night his hunger carries me
home from the farthest countries of sleep.
No footfall so secret I can't detect it,
no sack so dark I wouldn't climb in
to keep him safe till he finds his way.
Blind Death opens the sack by his crib,
and I leap in and fasten it closed.

He shakes me out in a prison of bones
and gives me a dustpan, bucket, and broom,
and sends me to clean the quarters of Death.
A pedestal anchors the Book of the Dead.
Turning the pages, I find my name.
In the opening letter, I see my son,
pack on his back, riding his crib,
and steering straight for my empty arms.

The next day I open the book.
Turning the pages I find my name,
In the second letter I see my son
spurring our old piano to heaven,
leaving the corpse of his broken crib.
Now he is passing the house of the moon.

MAN:    "Who comes here from the edge of the earth?
        I shall send my oceans and tides to drown
            him."

WOMAN:  The third day I open the book.
        In the last letter I see my child
        walking the sun's gold path on the water,
        the broken piano awash in his wake.
        That night the door of my cell flies open
        and he, his beauty weathered away,
        tumbles the bones and tugs at my skirt.

CHILD:                "Mother, mother,
        Climb on my back before the bones tell."

CONGREGATION:   *One of the living has rescued the dead!*

WOMAN:  The bones wake Death with whistling and
            drumming,
        and grabbing his net, he gallops down space.
        On the path of the sun, I see his shadow.
(*shouts*)  "Death is upon us! I feel his sting!"

CHILD:  "Throw him the apple I tucked in my pack.
        One side is morning, the other is night."

WOMAN:  Death gobbles the apple and bellows for more.

        At the house of the moon, I hear Death's heart.
        He whips my heels and opens the bag.
(*shouts*)  "Death is upon us! I feel his fingers!"

CHILD:  "Throw him the yo-yo I stuck in my pack.
        One side is shadow, the other is light."

WOMAN:  Death catches the yo-yo, it twinkles and spins,
        walks like a dog and whirls round the world,
        and nests like a sparrow, warming his hand.

At the edge of the earth, Death tosses his net.
His net is kindly and turns to a ship.
My child is tired and sleeps in the prow.
I do not tell him that Death has caught us,
he does not tell me Death will return.
He rattles his crib and learns to survive,
watching the clowns that teach us to fall,
hearing the angels that keep us alive.

1. Rainer Maria Rilke, *Letters to a Young Poet,* trans. M. D. Herter Norton (New York: W. W. Norton, 1954), pp. 66–67.
2. Joseph Campbell, *The Masks of God: Primitive Mythology* (New York: Viking Press, 1969), p. 118.
3. *Ibid.,* p. 252.
4. Isaiah 40: 6–8.
5. St. John 10: 9–11, 27–29.

WAYNE PROUDFOOT:

## Church and Community

Many in the youth culture have responded to modern society by embracing models of community which are holistic and which lie at the opposite extreme from the individualism of the liberal heritage. While these holistic models are celebrated as reflecting an expansion of consciousness, a feeling of oneness with the universe, and the expansion of possibilities beyond the hopes and dreams of previous generations, they may in fact reflect the necessity of conceiving the world as a system which is contained and in which harmony is essential for survival. It may be a response to a universe which is more closed than it has been previously, which offers fewer possibilities rather than more, and which demands that aspirations and behavior adjust themselves to a scarcity of resources and a constant proximity of persons that allows little room for conflict.

On the frontier, if a conflict developed between two strong egos, one could drive the other out of town ("This town's not big enough for both of us") or could himself leave to seek his fortune elsewhere. Conflicts within family or community could be escaped by throwing oneself into one's work. This course was respected by society. In the present state of overcrowding and of scarcity of opportunities for meaningful work, the young have realized, perhaps unconsciously, that they must develop adaptive procedures for a world in which these conditions prevail. No longer can one permit conflict to flare up in the assurance that there is always a safety valve, room for expansion or escape. Perhaps because there is no safe context for conflict, either international or familial, the new skills of conflict management and of sensitivity training have evolved. Persons are trained in groups whose only rule is that the group remain for a set period within a closed room and deal with whatever might arise without leaving that room. This image is an apt one for the condition in which society is increasingly finding itself.

The new holistic model may thus be a response to the loss of frontiers. The individual is no longer sovereign. Rather, that individuality which is competitive and encourages conflict may be dysfunctional and threaten to destroy the harmony and mutual cooperation that is needed for survival in a closed system. Individuality can be encouraged if it is not competitive and does not produce conflict. "Do your own thing" is understood to imply "as long as it does not encroach upon anyone else." The liberal political tradition also attempted to protect individuals from having their freedoms encroached upon by others, but in that context there was sufficient room for all. Puritans seeking freedom could come to the New World. Others could settle their own communities where they could govern themselves. In the increasingly closed world of the present, the prohibition against encroaching upon the territory of another is much more limiting because proximity is so great.

In reaction against the liberal notions of competition and achievement, the boundaries of community according to the holistic understanding are often ascribed according to criteria which intentionally frustrate any possibility of ranking by achievement. Consider the "community of Libras." Or the community of all the individuals who happened to be present at Woodstock or at any concert by the Grateful Dead. The feelings of community which are expressed here, or in the sharing of drugs and music among a group of strangers, are specifically suited to cut across any lines that might possibly be drawn by achievement. The attempt to turn to astrology or the *I Ching* for instruction regarding specific decisions is an explicit rejection of the autonomy of the individual. It is a dramatic portrayal, even if not taken completely seriously, of a desire for the individual to return to a state of security in which his or her activity is brought into harmony with the cosmos and he or she no longer has the responsibility of making independent decisions, of acting as an autonomous individual. All of these are attempts to ascribe governance to an external power rather than rooting it in the sovereignty of the individual, as is the case in the theory of the social contract.

From the holistic perspective, language is interpreted as, at best, an inadequate tool by which individuals attempt to express feelings. Language has always been a prime tool for discrimination. Much of the emphasis upon feeling, upon achieving unity with the cosmos is an attempt to blur discrimination. It is a longing to return to a holistic harmony with the implication that linguistic skills are rationalistic accouterments of a technological culture. The attempt is made to avoid the fine discriminations which language permits and may even entail, in order to adopt a nonlinguistic mode of awareness and feeling. The undifferentiated state of experience is celebrated and sought. The preference for the nonverbal over the verbal, for feeling over argument, for cosmic harmony over political decision is a preference for the undifferentiated whole over the exercise of powers of discrimination. Scientific or merely rational language which might be used for debate, for proposing hypotheses and articulating conflict is specifically rejected. Persons are enjoined to experience one another directly, without the medium of conventional knowledge of name, occupation, and the data which introductory conversation might reveal. Such immediate experience is impossible, however. When data are lacking concerning another person we tend to project and "read into" our experiences of that person sufficient data to fill in the blanks. The amount of information projected may be increased in the absence of the initial discrimination which language can provide. Music, drugs, the physical discipline of yoga and other aids to meditation are employed in an effort to transcend language and its power to discriminate. Language is interpreted as a weak substitute for "real" communication and experience.

The conception of time which accompanies this ideal of holistic harmony is one which involves a focus on present sensations. Again immediacy is the goal. Though immediacy is technically impossible, states of awareness such as those induced by drugs, meditation, music, and perhaps by boredom or television contribute to the emphasis on obliterating memory and anticipation. Life is to be lived in the present. Abjuring immediate gratification in order to obtain a future goal is discouraged. This may partly reflect the fact that this generation of youth sees no future. Certainly most adolescents today are not faced with the infinite future of open possibilities and opportunities which seemed to beckon a generation ago. Refuge is sought in the immediate. The celebration of present sensations discourages competition and conflict which might ensue if individuals fought each other for a diminishing set of opportunities.

Possibly the sharing of food and marijuana at a rock concert, the emphasis on cooperation rather than competition, the enjoyment of present gratification rather than working toward some goals in an uncertain future are adaptive forms of behavior in the present situation. A nation full of strong-willed heroes and frontiersmen could hardly survive in a society in which the frontiers are few and the boundaries are closing in.

The church, both in the local parish and on the campus, has always provided some form of community. The extent to which this community met the needs of its members depended upon its recognition of social and economic realities. In the nineteenth century when the culture sanctioned individual achievement it was not only the Calvinist ethic of salvation and its mundane rewards but also the evangelical insistence on individual decisions for Christ and on the conversion of each person that buttressed these sanctions. In the past the church has self-consciously considered itself to be a witnessing community to the power of freedom and self-sacrifice which was symbolized in the life of Jesus and which was proclaimed as a goal of the Christian community. To maintain a consonance with the present needs of society, the church must provide an active and flourishing community which can incorporate the compassion and cooperation demanded by the increasing population and the closing boundaries of our world, and which can at the same time provide the continuity for a sense of personal identity that is rooted in the past and projected toward the future. To attempt to return to a world where decisions are imposed by fate or the stars, where relations are ascribed rather than achieved, is to retreat to a position which might provide some gratification and security in the face of the present confusion, but which abandons all control over the future shape of our lives to forces that have already become inexorable. Only careful planning, cooperation, and the development of that discipline which requires the delay of gratification can provide for an open future and for the possibility of meaningful activity and the development of increasing levels of discrimination and the accompanying pleasures that can make the future attractive both for individuals and for communities.

For a period in Western Europe, Marxism seemed to offer a possibility for man to influence and shape his own future, and provided motivation for the kind of discipline which was necessary for that task. To many peoples in the world today, Marxism still offers the best analysis and model for man in relation to his future. However, the last few years have shown that closure is not due only to the economic oppression on which Marx focused. The children of the middle and upper classes of the most wealthy society in the world have also experienced this closure. When Marx called upon the proletariat to rise up and take control, there was still a sense of an infinitely expanding future in which would occur the inevitable progress from a capitalist economy to a classless society. Closure of the spirit now threatens to undermine the desire for self-determination and autonomy on which Marx was able to draw.

The holistic ideal of community and the preference for cooperation over competition is a necessary response to the conditions of the world and to the present individualism that is rooted in the economics of capitalism. But it may also be an insufficient and even a potentially harmful response if it involves the abandonment of discrimination and careful planning in favor of immediate sensation and celebration of the present. The church has always had a teleological thrust which has emphasized the necessity of planning together and cooperating to establish a more human society. It is important at this juncture for the church to represent a community in which the values of development, the identity of a people by virtue of a common history, and the necessity for individuals to plan together to achieve a more just and human society are present. In the establishment of this community the church has much to learn from experiments at cooperation represented by food co-ops, communal living arrangements, medical and legal services, and political caucuses among members of the new culture.

## Living the Kingdom

The experience which has had an increasingly powerful impact on our own lives has been our growing with and benefiting from a community of young Friends centered at New Swarthmoor Community, a commune in New York State. Founded by a group of young Friends, New Swarthmoor has become increasingly "interdenominational," and has proved to be of real meaning to several Brethren, Mennonites, and a variety of people who never expected anything remotely "religious" to be of value to them.

New Swarthmoor combines many things we wouldn't believe would work, except that we've seen the community work fairly well over a period of approximately two years. Included in it are people with very different religious beliefs: those who believe in thorough study and use of the Bible, and those who reject almost completely hymn singing and the use of the Bible. There are people with different political beliefs, people going to and from the physical location of New Swarthmoor at a very high turnover rate, no private rooms, and no turning away of people for lack of space or compatibility. The entire community picks up and moves to where the trial of a draft resister is occurring, or to Washington for various nonviolent direct actions. Income-sharing occurs: no record is kept of where money comes from, and people are free to take what they feel they need.

Most of the money comes from apple-picking, which many people in the community spend two months doing each autumn. This money goes directly to the New Swarthmoor income pool. This is generally the only work they do for money during the year. The rest of the time they are free to follow the leadings of the Spirit, which may mean traveling around to different Quaker gatherings to witness to their beliefs, getting involved in nonviolent direct action, and spending time at New Swarthmoor in worship, religious study, and maintenance of the life of the community through working in the garden, doing repairs on the house and grounds, and baking bread.

Emphasis is placed on the concept of "simplicity," and members are continually seeking ways to simplify their lives; for them this means a wood-burning stove for heating, outhouses and no indoor plumbing, vegetarian meals consisting mainly of dried beans, their own organic-garden produce, and homemade bread and peanut butter, which are all cheaper than cheese and eggs. All of these things also produce a closer link with what it takes to maintain one's life. The community is very close to being self-sustaining because it spends very little money on things which other Americans consider to be necessities. For example, often wood which someone has cut down and cannot use is given to them to burn in the winter.

A real effort is made to be aware of the roles that men and women are taking and to share responsibilities as equally as possible. Men have really learned to cook and often volunteer to do it, while women share in heavy work and are beginning to learn how to repair machines. Both women and men take leadership roles in the spiritual and business life of the community.

We feel this is all possible because of the very strong spiritual base for everything the community does. Worship is central to the life of New Swarthmoor, and occurs most days in a somewhat planned, somewhat spontaneous fashion. The daily life emphasizes seeking for what is right for individuals and for the group in community life. The concept of "clearness committee" has been revived from early Quakerism. The Clearness Committee usually meets in the spirit of worship, and people ask questions about a decision facing some individual to help that person become clear about what she or he should do. The group helps seek for the right answer, but it is still up to the individual to make the final decision. Clearness committees have met to help people in their decisions about whether to continue in graduate school, whether to continue on probation (for draft resistance) or refuse that and go to jail, what kind of vocation to follow, what is right for a particular individual to do about sexuality, and many other topics.

Decisions about community life are made in essentially the same way, with the entire group making up the Clearness Committee. Out of the silence of worship, individuals share their leadings about the appropriate choice for the group to make when faced with some decision. All are encouraged to share their concerns, and from the mutual sharing, a consensus, tested by silent worship and consideration, is usually reached. Believing strongly that there is something of God in every woman and man, the group tries to be open to leadings of the Spirit of God possibly coming at strange times and in unusual ways.

The importance of worship in keeping the community together is borne out by the fact that when the spiritual life lacks depth (and New Swarthmoor does have its ups and downs, just as other groups do), the people of different religious beliefs do not get along and have petty arguments. But when the Spirit is really there none of that seems to matter, and they begin to understand each other.

With New Swarthmoor Community we have discovered far more powerful spiritual experiences than usually oc-

curred in traditional Meetings for Worship (a scheduled
worship service on Sunday morning, consisting of silence
and speaking when one is moved by the Spirit). We have
had intense, spontaneous Meetings for Worship at many
times and places, and with all kinds of things occurring: silence, reading, talking, singing, dancing, arrests, trials, and
"quaking," all very much as awareness of the Spirit.

The community believes in listening seriously for leadings of the Spirit, testing them, and *living* them. This spiritual power came to bear on the spring, 1971, political actions in Washington, D.C., and led there to instance after
instance of the most powerful and living nonviolent direct
action we have ever seen and participated in.

We want briefly to describe nonviolent direct action as
founded in the Gandhian philosophy of nonviolence, or
*satyagraha* (better translated as "truth-power" than "non-
violence"). Such a description is important because nonviolent direct action is frequently misunderstood, and because its philosophy has become increasingly important to
us as a way of living our beliefs.

A group utilizing *satyagraha* as a means for bringing
about social change practices first the principle of *truth-
seeking*. For Gandhi, and for us, the nearest approach to
truth is trying unceasingly to love one's sisters and brothers. Pragmatically, truth-seeking means always keeping in
mind the fact that no one has a monopoly on truth. Specifically, the persons with whom one is contending in
trying to bring about some social change may well have
some of the truth, and communication with them should
be maintained at all times. One who practices *satyagraha*
(i.e., a *satyagrahi*) should always be ready for the possibility of being convinced that the change he or she thought

was desirable actually is not, or at least that it should be pursued in some very different way.

A second key principle flows from the first: *nonviolence,* or action based on the refusal to do harm. No one can be sure of possessing enough truth to justify hurting or killing another in the name of truth. When one's goal is truth, one's means must be loving and truthful; the means must not violate the ends. One doesn't achieve world peace by making war, or bring about lasting social change by silencing an "opponent" with a show of force.

A steadfast commitment to social change set in a context of truth-seeking and refusal to do harm leads to the principle of *self-suffering.* Makers of social change have frequently said, in effect, "This change is so important that I'm willing to make *you* suffer and perhaps die for it." The *satyagrahi* says, "This change is so important that *I'm* willing to suffer and perhaps die for it."

In summary, a nonviolent campaign for social change is characterized by a combination of open, loving communication with everyone involved (hence an absence of secrecy), a refusal to hurt anyone, and a persistence in achieving the goal that may, if necessary, pass through discussion and attempts at negotiation, efforts to educate the relevant population about the issue, pickets, boycotts, strikes, sit-ins, fasts, imprisonment, and sometimes death.

What follows is a good case study for a nonviolent action living up fairly well to the principles we have outlined.

During April, 1971, New Swarthmoor formed the organizing core, and set the tone for, a demonstration at the national headquarters of the Selective Service System. The goal of the demonstration was to get large numbers of people into the SSS building to talk with employees there about the implications of their jobs, connections to the war, etc. Good communication with SSS Director Curtis Tarr and other officials was established several weeks in advance, and when at the last moment we were refused entry to talk with employees, the demonstration remained completely nonviolent, all the way through the arrest of the last of the 225 demonstrators. The religious tone infused into the action really made a difference to everyone involved. Those arrested, the employees of Selective Service, the policemen, jailers, and those trying us in court all felt the impact of this religious witness, and we ourselves felt its strength and rightness.

Also in this action were some concrete examples of the equality possible in the roles women and men take. In the trial, where we defended ourselves rather than having a lawyer, women were prominent in asking questions of the witnesses and going to see the judge in his chambers. These acts conveyed a very different tone from that set by the traditional male lawyer who defended some of our sisters and brothers being tried with us.

A demonstration of such character might not have been possible if there hadn't been a community existing for about a year ahead of time which laid the spiritual base and pulled a loose community of about fifty people together. The loving impact we had on Selective Service employees is well illustrated by the fact that a number of them raised bail money for us, and a high-ranking official testified in our behalf at our trial. This experience strengthened our conviction that it is not only possible but necessary for a fully committed spiritual search to wrestle with the problems of the world. This still means to us that one must strive at all times simply to do what is right, rather than giving primary consideration to questions of effectiveness or expediency. Living the kingdom of God and loving your fellow woman and man means confronting and overcoming fear, not retreating from frightening situations.

To move on from the concrete example, we would like to discuss the following question: What is the future of religious seekings of young people and how can concerned, religiously motivated persons relate constructively to them? We feel that the appropriate response of concerned persons to these seekings is to help the experimenting young to achieve something lastingly meaningful, which may provide valuable models for the majority of youth who tend to see the spiritual dimension of their lives as less than crucial. What this actually means in terms of doing is all of us learning to *live* our beliefs, and letting the quality of our lives show kids we care about them. One way adults can help is in dealing with the conservative institutional religious structures we have found present in all organized religion. In our work with young people of many denominations, we have found that institutionalized Quakerism and Catholicism, for example, usually include distressing amounts of authoritarianism and put up many roadblocks for young people trying to make changes in their own lives or the world. Thus Quaker and Catholic schools usually lack the concept of young people being able to control their own lives, to experiment, or to make changes in their environment. When young people are seeking changes and run up against these roadblocks, it is often crucial that they be given some help, some reason for hope. Failure at such a time might mean a choice for retreat, through drugs or other escapism, from what they see as a hopeless world. It is important to help them make a choice for *life,* for a continuation in working to see their ideals realized.

Really serving young people may mean making services available as needed: draft counseling, contraceptive counseling, help with runaways, bad drug trips, counseling in vocations for social change, conflict resolution, and nonviolent direct action. Living one's beliefs *may* also mean income-sharing, trying actively to make our roles as women and men more equitable and loving, living in a commune, beginning to dismantle the bureaucratic structure of our offices, and doing our own secretarial work. Secretaries and wives are in this culture treated as nameless interchangeable objects attachable to any handy male name, such as "Bob's secretary" or "Mrs. John Smith." We feel that people should type their own letters; in organizations which are trying to create changes in our society or become more Christian, everyone would have a more meaningful job if they did their own secretarial work. Neither a person dictating lots of letters nor a person typing someone else's letters and never getting any credit for the work enjoys it much; each would probably be more creative in writing his or her own letters *and* typing them.

Living the kingdom here and now is a difficult process and one which continues—it cannot be done at one stroke. What's needed for all of us is ways of being more and more open to the Spirit, and living Truth and Love more and more fully. We feel that kids can tell pretty well when someone comes to them in a spirit of love and respect for them as persons. The experience of New Swarthmoor people in finding that their community is felt to be extremely meaningful, even by people who think of themselves as nonreligious, is a strong case in point.

It is probably more difficult to learn how to, and to try to, take a participatory democratic approach to community and God, than to become a faceless, obedient believer in a cult, sect, or church which claims to have all the answers and demands unquestioning agreement (i.e., Jesus freaks and Baba lovers, who must obey elders or gurus). People often need the support of a place like New Swarthmoor to grow into a real seeking approach; once they learn the joy and strength in it, most are extremely unwilling to go back into the authoritarian structures that make up most of society.

We must all search the new and the old forms of religious seeking for the principles that will point us toward long-range solutions of life problems. For the two of us, the philosophy of nonviolence has become increasingly important, especially the idea that no one has a monopoly on the Truth and the allied idea that there is that of God in every human being.

Live the kingdom!

## Spiritual Quest on a State University Campus

Sometimes I feel embarrassed to be a professor at a state university: presence and participation, no matter how subversive, do contribute to the maintenance of an odious system; the students whom I see most are white and middle class; it's easy for me to think of myself as a talker, not a doer. For this state of mind, the alternatives that present themselves are to burn it down; go do something else; or try to build a better kind of school.

When squarely faced, the alternatives *for me so far* seem less constructive than what I'm doing. The state university, as many have observed, is the state church of modern times. Most young people have to pass this way. It cannot be burned down unless the society is burned down, although one or more individual temples can be closed at great cost to the students and some temporary inconvenience to the state. Those who postulate new and freer forms of learning—Margaret Mead, Ivan Illich, Judson Jerome—are offering exciting alternatives which, I am convinced, will not be generally available in my time, no matter what I do. As for the students being white and middle class, these are, after all, my people; nobody is making concessions to them, however things may appear; and they are in great need. Working with them, bridging with them the gap between books and reality, words and communication, is doing.

Established churches and state schools have common ills and common duties. They suffer from standardization, repression, traditionalism, rigidity. Yet their chief duty (incredibly enough) is to teach and celebrate participation in life, which is dynamic. Such participation and celebration can be achieved in two interrelated ways: by the fostering of individual creativity, through love and knowledge of self, and God in self; and by the establishment of communion, through knowledge, respect, and love of others, and informed participation in God's human community, past and present. My intention here is to dwell primarily on the problems and possibilities in achieving these goals within the state university, with briefer comments on what the campus church can contribute. Although my discussion can only be from personal knowledge, I hope it will not sound arrogant: the teacher is much less important than the attitude and the method, which anyone who has the time can employ.

Some of the idols of the state university as reflected in the teaching of English literature (and, I suppose, most of the humanities) are *objectivity, covering ground, knowing the best that has been thought and said,* and *expository prose.* In practice, *objectivity* (written into my faculty rule book) assumes that it is irrelevant, dangerous, and immoral to be swayed by likes or dislikes, and thereby denies the realities of preference, differing tastes and needs, and even enjoyment (as opposed to "appreciation"). *Covering ground* assumes the superior importance of quantitative knowledge, familiarity with a range of names and dates as opposed to intensive and perhaps passionate involvement with, say, one or two authors in a given period. *The best that has been thought and said* assumes the centrality and continuing static primacy of a limited tradition in Western culture. And *expository prose* (plagiarized or otherwise, drudgery almost always) assumes that only one kind of response to literature is acceptable within the academic framework. To such an extent have these shibboleths overtaken common sense that my department at its annual soul-searching session, anxious to be tolerant of rebels, passed consecutive motions stating that thinking is important, but writing is essential.

Certification (B.A. or whatever) may be equivalent to confirmation or admission to church membership; the university, however, aggressively excludes the "unworthy" in its barrages of tests and grades, its relentless surveillance of student behavior, its punitive housing conditions, its endless red tape, its excessive and absurd academic requirements, and its random exclusion of students from overcrowded required courses. In this sterile wilderness, many students literally can see no meaning to any of the tasks they have to perform: studying Hawthorne makes no more sense than standing in line. Everything turns them into passive receptacles with little or no power to control their own destinies. (A Columbus, Ohio, judge, sentencing some students who had agitated for reform, argued that you buy a ticket to see an education show, not to put on the show.) Course grades seem as accidental as being let into the course to begin with, and under these circumstances plagiarism is as reasonable a way to satisfy requirements as trying unsuccessfully to figure out "what the teacher wants."

Things would not seem so bad if the students were not so good. Except for size, which after a while makes an important qualitative difference, the same complaints could have been leveled against the universities for years. But whereas previously most students merely wanted the security that goes with certification, now they are more painfully sensitive to other needs and more desperately anxious to learn how to live. Compared to young people of only a short time ago, they are extraordinarily open, serious, uncompetitive, moral, religious, and in need of community. What has struck me hardest this year is the recognition that their openness has not even brought them community among themselves. All it seems to have done is to stimulate reactions for them or against them, as if they thought they knew all the answers, as if they have something all set up that can be either ratified or opposed.

The assumption that they have a code of life pleasing to them is particularly dangerous, since it polarizes unproductively. The students have no more answers than we do. They have only need, and some underlying convictions about how things should or should not be done. They find themselves so fragmented, so busy with meaningless tasks, that they have almost no way to talk to people, to avoid making mistakes, or to learn how to be themselves. Furthermore, they have heard too many misleading words from ministers, professors, and politicians, and with no education adequate to help them recognize rhetorical sincerity, their tendency is to reject words altogether. Spiritual fulfillment is an obvious defense against the mechanical traps of the world, but they don't know how to find it.

The professor concerned with spiritual quest can try to confront the university with a meaningful version of itself. The American anxiety to deny official sanction to any creed or value system has exhibited the defect of its virtue by its contribution to an ideal of value-free learning, learning for its own sake, stripped of any regard for immediate usefulness or felt need. The present combination of extreme need for meanings with rejection of imposed beliefs suggests that every congregation and every class must become a community banded together to discover what truths it needs for itself, defended by its communal nature both from coercion from without and from mere anarchy within. Further, communal learning is itself an experience:

it reunites words with meaning, facts with self-knowledge, learning with life. On the basis of this year's experimentation, I believe that the establishment of such communities, temporary though they must be, is the single most important thing that either church or faculty can do about the religious and intellectual welfare of students, at least in huge universities, such as the midwestern one where I teach. They cling to the experience and to each other: my most recent class is meeting without me through the summer. Several students, asked how these courses are different from others, have said, "This is part of my life."

Such communality can only with the greatest difficulty be achieved in a traditional classroom. Mocking our supposed sense of the vitality of what we do, we have never questioned the appropriateness of officiating in rooms that are barren imitations of Protestant churches, which are barren enough to begin with. Typically, we have a rectangular space, people sitting in rows of fixed chairs, a raised platform at one end from which we may hold forth, a podium from which the word may be intoned, a blackboard upon which it may be written.

This year I broke all my classes into groups small enough to meet in my office (which has in it a rug but no desk) or at home. Everything was voluntary except participation in the group (unless the student chose to work by independent reading, or, as has not yet happened, part of the class voted not to accept this method of doing things). A wide range of possible individual or group projects was suggested, including exams and papers; nothing was required. The final grade (unfortunately, under our system a letter grade has to be given) was arrived at by consultation between teacher and student, with the student having the last word. A student under this system could theoretically do nothing and get an "A," and many people expected that most students would in this way "take advantage" of the teacher. Such an attitude assumes that there's a war on; we found that when the grade ceased to be a weapon, the students were freed of all kinds of resentment and resistance and became able to take learning seriously for its own sake. They found themselves spending more time on this than on other courses because they were doing it for themselves. And a sense of mutual responsibility took hold; they saw that each of them was needed to make the seminar work, and the idea of being needed was in itself of memorable importance to them.

My failure to require expository prose has been especially distressing to some of my colleagues, yet I have found that its power of alienation far exceeds its value. Good critical writing delighted my generation because it was still the access to a real community of scholars. Now it is increasingly a solitary activity, destined to a meaninglessly competitive system of artificial, generally unread publication. For students (most of whom nowadays have no intention even of going to graduate school), it is entirely solitary, related only by a competitive grade scale to the unseen papers of their colleagues. They see no reason whatever to do it; for them it is no more useful than reciting fifty "Hail Mary's" and probably less so. Although most of us have been deadened to the possibility of realizing such an obvious fact, writing is not the only way to respond to art. It is, in fact, one of the least obvious ways to do it.

Given the chance to spend their time reading and thinking, the students engaged in continuously interesting and often exciting class discussions. Sharing their ideas with their colleagues was a unique experience for them and it became its own reward. Released from fear of failure, they were also able to experiment with a wide and impressive variety of creative expression: abstract paintings and photographs to illustrate poems; a production of Milton's *Comus*, with music, dancing, costumes, and backdrops; a historical novel set in the seventeenth century, for which the author used information he had picked up in almost every one of his college courses; much poetry; some expository prose; a concert of Renaissance music; and some interesting journals relating the literature to the students' own experience. No longer having to compete with one another (a procedure which they almost all detest), or mechanically repeat the same predictable routines, they found themselves able to live up to themselves, even to parts of themselves of which they had been unaware. I believe that this experience of self-fulfillment (which could almost always be shared enjoyably with the group) complements the communality which I have described earlier, and that both together can play a significant part in spiritual quest.

I have been asked to explain how Shakespeare and Milton can be made interesting to students. The method accounts for much, though certainly not all. It seems to me that the real problem with tradition is not that students reject the whole past because it's past, but because it has been presented to them as though all its separate parts are equally indispensable at all times, and as though its values are transcendent and static—"the best that has been thought and said." If that were true, then I suppose people couldn't be educated at all, but only trained. We need to see the value of tradition as, like God, immanent and dynamic. We need to make our curriculum more free-swinging, to present themes and problems rather than literary periods, and to learn enough sensitivity to students from year to year to know what is going to be useful to them. The value even of any particular play by Shakespeare is always questionable. There are all kinds of beautiful furniture in this world, but if any one kind does not fit into the house I now occupy, it would be foolish of me to buy it. It would be good for me to know how to get a furniture catalog in case I should remodel my house or buy a new one (and *some* exposure to new furniture may motivate me to remodel my house), but right now I need what I can eat off and sleep on in the house I have: Kenneth Burke valuably calls literature "equipment for living." [1] That is what for too long it has not been.

So far, while a number of Renaissance writers are of questionable present usefulness, Shakespeare and Milton continue to compel. Milton is a particularly good example of a figure who can be made to seem very remote or else very immediate, and much that Milton talks about relates to what we are trying to do: a religious revolutionary, he saw freedom as an inner need of all men. He believed that the purpose of education is to repair the ruins of our first parents. Thus, teaching Milton in an atmosphere of enjoyment and wholeness is, to begin with, doing what we're reading about—which is often the case when education is going well. The process and the aim become one.

*Paradise Lost* is an epic poem about how Satan waged war in heaven and got thrown into hell, and then came to earth and corrupted Adam and Eve into disobedience and punishment. But no great poem is that dogmatic, though it has been treated as though its content were obvious. It took a radical critic in our time to argue that "Milton thought he was writing to enable personal redemption and social revolution; we note merely that he revived certain epic devices." [2] The poem is mythic. Its meaning widens under close reading until one sees this: that God is life, Satan's rebellion is denial of life, the Son of God is creative love, Adam and Eve "imparadis't in one another's arms" are man's ideal wholeness—integrity of intellect and imagination, male and female, and so forth. The fall is a fall into self-consciousness and self-dividedness, signaled by their decision to separate in order to get more work done without distracting each other by their happiness. Part of original sin turns out to bring on what we think of as the Puritan ethic—work separated from play.

A major problem for students is that Milton's parochial language, which appears at first glance to convey very traditional religious notions, was the only way he knew to express universal truths. Likewise, the Book of Common Prayer, even in revised form, is full of language that must to some extent be reinterpreted. Milton was ahead of his time, and ahead of the Prayer Book too, in getting into his language the concept of an evolutionary God, a God immanent as well as transcendent, a ground-of-our-being. A student who discovers how to read Milton in this way simultaneously recognizes some of the value of the past, rethinks his religious views, and learns to appreciate the poet. But these things can't be achieved *ex cathedra*. Milton's poetry is very aggressive and argumentative: it's made, if any poetry ever was, for just the kind of lively, intense discussion which can't take place in an impersonal lecture hall.

It can't take place, either, under a pedagogical system that (as did our pseudo-scientific "new criticism") ignores the humanity of Milton (or even of Milton's God). The man was a political radical who had to make a series of agonizing political-moral decisions during the middle twenty years of his life, and who indeed gave up writing poetry all that time because he had believed that Utopia could be achieved in England. Such problems as the following arose: Milton finally had to recognize that most of the English people wanted the restoration of the monarch, wanted to live under what he considered tyranny. What does one do when the minority is right? Milton's view is that the minority should force its will on the majority. One cannot, when teaching undergraduates, simply analyze this argument as a rhetorical exercise; you have to let them work through it, see its strengths and fallacies, apply it to their own experience, and come to their own conclusions, together and separately, about its validity. For these students a central problem of *Samson Agonistes* is very similar: Samson is right; therefore he has a right to commit wholesale slaughter upon the Philistines in order to free his people from bondage. It is just not possible to try simply to make students accept the historical context of all that. Once Milton becomes present to them as a real person, they have a right to judge him both in his own context and for his significance to theirs. He would have wanted that too.

Paul Goodman speaks of our time as a New Reformation.[3] The central issue of the sixteenth-century Reformation was the right of the people to read and interpret the Bible for themselves. This is what for so long we have not allowed our students or our congregations really to do. The teacher's interpretation has been right, unless (sometimes) the student could devise a better case for his own reading. It is time for the reassertion of the concept of the priesthood of the believer. That is dangerous stuff. It is easy to throw the baby out with the bath. And that is why I come back again and again to the essential nature of communal learning. The student is no longer willing to take my word for anything, nor can I accept his. All we have is the risky but reasonable hope that as a group, getting to know each other's individual strengths and weaknesses, we can perhaps trust ourselves. And knowing me as a person who has put herself at their disposal, who in some sense they can choose or not choose to elect as leader, they do trust and use me more productively (I think) than when they used to write down notes to use on midterms and finals.

So, on this campus of 45,000 people, there are, here and there, opportunities for community, fragmented, time-bound, frustratingly inadequate as they must be. What can the campus ministry do? It already does a lot of things of which I am aware: it houses and encourages free university classes; it assists draft resistance; to some extent, it makes community for students who are church-minded to begin with. Surely there must be campuses where everything I can think of is already being done. But the following to me are crying needs.

The churches, individually and through agencies like the Church Society for College Work, can give their lay professors help and support in making learning communities in their classrooms. These efforts take enormous energy, they are apt to meet severe opposition from other faculty members and administrators, and it is very easy for the teacher under these circumstances to lose perspective—to think himself either misguided or heroic. He needs counsel and support to keep him steady.

Exposing himself to the young as people, the faculty member must find himself open to all that appeals to them, including new life-styles. The young are more flexible, but they also are torn between old and new. As with ways of learning, those who seem to side with the young are likely to be herded with them into arbitrary categories and forced to adopt moral stances of which they are very unsure. In my experience, with the exception of draft resistance, the church is totally unprepared to give relevant moral counsel on contemporary problems. If the church can't do it, who can?

Here as elsewhere, students want from the church what they can use as equipment for living; the church must go to them to find out what that is. Any church they can trust will have to have people of visible spiritual commitment at its center, people whose religion has given them courage to be real and happy. They need a human, available Jesus. Serious thought needs to be given to the concept of an evolutionary God whose working is limited by the limitedness of the lives through which he works. The church must be willing to give up its power to such a God, to accept the fact that the Spirit is often most vividly manifest in its youngest members, and to facilitate whatever can let that Spirit loose in the world as a changing and renewing force, to the end that Christian people need not merely stand against society but may hope to let God remake it through them. Church architecture, like classroom architecture, is almost totally damaging at present. Churches, like classrooms, ought to be dynamic places, where people can see each other and feel alive. Church language and theology, too, need to be remodeled toward the concept of inner vitality and away from the old opposition of God's transcendence to man's unworthiness.

The great ecclesiastical gifts, for which there are no other explicit sources and no reliable ones, are celebration, communion, and help with personal salvation in a godless world. Suicide is a major cause of death among teenagers just because they see no reason for celebration and have no sense of community or hope of salvation. They live (and always have) in such an immediate way that salvation has to be now (as it should be), not tomorrow morning. If the church can't show believably that it cares about the life of every sparrow and that life now is valuable and joyous, then it ought to shut up shop.

The establishment of the church as the active life of the Spirit in the world does not require any particular pattern of external trappings, and to become overconcerned with appearances may be to lose God. But I would suppose that such a church as I have described might be disposed to trade in black (or purple) robes, solemn intonations, and endless confessions of guilt, for bright vestments and clothes, banners and bells, joyous hymns, guitars and drums. Instead of the already obsolete licensed layreaders, there should be real communion of saints with as full participation as possible from everyone. There should always be passing of communion from hand to hand; establishment of more traditions like the Peace, where people can acknowledge each other; constant liturgical innovation, with people always free to make their own prayers and services, especially in a communal way. Tradition is essential; but people need to see that tradition as dynamic, not static; they need to see that they can make it as well as share in it.

If the church were a place where people could really go to renew themselves, then the charge at the end of the service, to go forth into the world, might come to mean something. Christ said in one of his most brilliant and memorable utterances that he came to give us abundant life. Obviously the church has life around, somewhere or other, but too often that life is so hidden or warped or even turned against itself as to repel the uninitiate. All the church needs to do is to allow the vitality of the Word to become visible. Most ministers feel restrained by the expectations of conservative congregations. The campus ministry has the enormous asset of at least a potential congregation that is flexible, eager, and aware. Students have more existence than they can handle; they crave life. A church that exhibited abundant life would not need to ask how to attract or help the young.

1.  Kenneth Burke, "Literature as Equipment for Living," *The Philosophy of Literary Form* (2nd ed.; Baton Rouge: Louisiana State University Press, 1967).

2.  Jackie DiSalvo, "This Murder: Literary Criticism and Literary Scholarship," *NUC-MLC Newsletter*, I, 11.

3.  Paul Goodman, *New Reformation; Notes of a Neolithic Conservative* (New York: Random House, 1970).

DANIEL BURKE:

## New Dimensions of the Spiritual Quest

Running through all the turmoil of the present is an implicit question which relates entirely to the matter of spiritual quest. The question is, "Where will we find the resources to deal with the problems and tasks that confront us?" With our technology, which can deliver a man within a few hundred feet of a target on the moon, we certainly have the means of distributing the goods of the earth. Where will we find the intentional ingredients to do so? With the basic instrumentalities of our democracy we have the means to distribute and balance power. What shall we draw upon to produce the will to accomplish this? We are haunted by the unremitting notion that life is or should be worthwhile. Where will we find ways to express this? Will they be inclusive as well as exclusive? And where shall we find the clues that enable us to know best when to include and when to exclude? There is a vast range of questions and problems for which there are no technical solutions.[1] How, then, do we deal with them?

This is the area of life out of which religions in general and the church in particular arose. The current spiritual quest may have dimensions to it that have never before been articulated, but it is still the work of the church to concern itself with these issues. No matter how badly compromised by racial, cultural, and economic considerations, the gospel remains as something that is both universal in its scope and particular in its address to each human being. With respect to the particular picture of today's spiritual quest that I have drawn, it seems to me that the church has only to do its time-honored tasks, theology and ethics.

Theology, at its best as I understand it, affirms both the rational and the mysterious. It affirms that there is One who is both keeper and revealer of the mystery over which existence is slung. In so doing, it guards the very mystery it seeks to comprehend. The leap of faith may be, as Kierkegaard pointed out, an either/or decision. But the faith itself is a both/and proposition. The heart of Christianity, the assertion that in Christ God became man does not separate out. Just because we cannot define exactly what incarnation constitutes does not prove that it has no meaning. This is where our positivist, analytical thrust begins to play us false. Definition has a way of becoming dogmatic certainty with us. No matter how many times our history reminds us that we transcend our terms, our legitimate need to take a fix on things overwhelms us in an endless series of idolatries. The God who is in but not of the world is a constant reminder of the similar dimensions of our own humanity, the constant undoer of our fixations. This embracing of opposites like "in but not of" is a prime characteristic of Eastern religions and one of the chief reasons for their popularity today. It is also at the center of our heritage—being what it always has been, a stumbling block to the strict monotheist and a scandal to the polytheist or humanist in us.

Theology, if it is to be useful to the contemporary quest, must explore this sense of fusion. The discipline of inclusiveness, with all of its bewildering ambiguity, rings too true to life to be ignored. Rationality and mystery, the one and the many, the absolute and the relative all belong and find their completion in one another. From our dialectic we must fashion a theology that synthesizes. To fashion such a theology means that we will have to relate our terms and symbols to the more profound and effective insights of contemporary life. For instance, theologically speaking, it can be pointed out that living in uncertainty is quite consonant with allegiance to God. A sense of what this means is not unimportant in an age and for a people as thoroughly relativized as ours. From the story of Abraham, who was urged to leave his familiar surroundings behind him, to the wide assortment of statements assailing and prohibiting idolatry, the picture of faith that emerges from the biblical narrative bears a striking resemblance to the most creative contemporary attitudes. From Werner Heisenberg, who enunciated the uncertainty principle (that interesting fusion of opposites):

For in those branches of science in which we have found that our knowledge is "suspended in mid-air," in just those branches we achieved a crystal clear understanding of the relevant phenomena. This knowledge is so transparent and carries with it such force of conviction that scientists of the most diverse peoples and races have accepted it as the undoubted basis of all further thought and cognition. Of course, we also make mistakes in science and it may take some time before they are found and corrected. But we can rest assured that there will be a final decision as to what is right and wrong. The decision will not depend on the belief, race, or origin or the scientists, but it will be taken by a higher power and will then apply to all men for all times.[2]

Compare this, in type if not necessarily in content, with Isaiah saying (43: 18–19, RSV):

> Remember not the former things,
> nor consider the things of old.
> Behold, I am doing a new thing;
> Now it springs forth, do you not perceive it?
> I will make a way in the wilderness,
> and rivers in the desert.

It should be noted in both cases that this is not a vacuous but an expectant suspension of belief. Vacuity and despair may well be a part of our response as we are stripped of our idols, but the overriding note is one of hope or trust. There are those times when not knowing can be more important for us than knowing. To use Yeats's metaphor, even the center may not hold, but the result is not necessarily mere anarchy. It can as easily be that new creation struggling to be born from the inexhaustible source for which we have no more adequate name than God. Living with that God means being as prepared to move as to stay, as prepared to relinquish as to cling to belief. You can get high probabilities often enough, but you can never be absolutely sure which is coming next. Our age, like any other, is an incredible clutter of such a trusting attitude and the most gross and banal idolatries. The task of theology is to keep alive the work of differentiation.

The biblical tirades against idolatry were not so much, as we tend to imagine, a matter of fearing the outrage of an offended deity. Rather, the concern was that when people gave their allegiance to idols, they automatically thereby sold their humanity short. Worshiping the baals with their cult of fertility and their horizons extending no further than the rise and fall of the seasons was a dead end. It is hardly true that fertility and the rounds of time are unimportant. But a fixation there meant that people lost track of some vital truths about themselves. They lost track of the sense that they were commissioned as stewards with some real dominion in creation; not to be votaries of nature but to master it and use it well. They lost track of that Abrahamic sense of movement and destiny that is conscious of life as an ongoing story. This is the sense that ultimately breaks the bonds of endless cycles and constitutes a uniquely human attribute. In short, they lost track of their humanity. The prophets saw quite clearly that what humans do flows from what they believe or what they worship. And so the ultimate outcome of idolatry is all manner of immorality. Actions which could be defended or justified within the small confines and penultimate concerns of idol worship simply would not stand up to the larger claims staked out in the worship of Israel's God. To be sure, this faith was read quite parochially at times. Israel's election became a possession to be defined like any other holding. But the prophets or, if you will, the theologians, did not shrink from applying their critique to their own human group. The seeds of Israel's faith are universal in their scope (cf. also the kingdom parables of the New Testament) even though their application often enough begins at home.

Parenthetically, it is not always the theologians who will be doing the important work in differentiating the idols and God; indeed, they will often be found opposing it. That too has precedence in biblical and church history, with the crucifixion standing at the vortex.

But we are asked what the church can do in the contemporary spiritual quest, and one of the answers is that it can do this ancient work of theology. Despite the passage of thousands of years, the issue of idolatry is very much with us today. The gods may not be made of silver, gold, stone, or wood (although there are Swiss banks, Kimberley mines, and the property fetish), but they can be all the more dangerous for that. Regard the number of people or institutions making the messianic claim, "You are either with me or against me." Left, right, or center they begin with a just criticism and end with a divisive self-righteousness. Or consider the ascendancy of technique in this most technological of all ages. Life is understood as so many subtle or unsubtle manipulations of bread. In this schema human beings tend to become objects to be quantified, shuffled, and processed by the makers of political economy. Such inversion of priorities lends itself perfectly to messianic demagoguery, to the erosion of any meaningful authority, and ultimately to a dissolution which destroys the just with the unjust. The Bible has a phrase for this; it is called "the wrath of God," which is the other side of the coin of human futility. It is not a fashionable thing to talk about in erudite circles, but when one considers the disasters with which we are flirting, and the stubbornness with which we cling to fatuities of rhetoric that cover despoiling and murderous actions, it is not too strong a description of our experience. And above all, what theology must strive to do is to relate its language, its insights, and its symbols to our experience.

The most obvious of the ways in which theology relates to experience is via the medium of ethics. Indeed, biblically speaking, theology and ethics are all of a piece. It is no accident, therefore, that we find the prohibition of idolatry at the top of the list of the Decalogue. It is stated more positively in the Shema, or in the summary of the law, but in either case, the beginning of ethics is seen to reside in worship. Our actions flow from our worship; what we value determines what we do. The framework for doing ethics resides in the prolegomena to the Ten Commandments. "I am the Lord your God, who brought you out of the land of Egypt, and out of the house of bondage." In the context of history, and a historical episode of deliverance at that, the children of Israel are admonished not to submit themselves to anything or anyone that can be encompassed by their art or imagination. In that light they can then make sense of a series of injunctions which enable them to take each other's existence as seriously as they take their own. There is a sense of enablement to the commandments which is badly eroded by the imperative tone. Loving or paying attention to God is both a thing in and of itself and yet inseparably linked to our relationship with each other.

The fact that paying attention to God is the best preparation for a true realization of ourselves and of our kindred creatures indicates an order of precedence that remains instructive today. In identifying and shunning idolatries in our history we may be able to construct life in manners which make it unnecessary to betray trust or take away our neighbor's reputation or property or life or to consume ourselves craving after the same. The delineation of meaning of terms like "adultery," "false witness," "stealing," and even "murder" will vary over time and often from situation to situation. We all know of contexts in which lying to protect the innocent from tyranny is not false witness. We know enough of the oedipal situation to allow a range of meanings in the business of honoring father and mother. We know also that honoring in families is a two-way street and that the concept of what constitutes a family changes over time. We know that respectable business arrangements can in reality be organized thievery. We know, in short, that the terms are ambiguous as to specifications. But we also know that their intent is clear. As basic touchstones for morality, the items in the Decalogue have stood the test of time pretty well. Like the generalities of any basic statement from the Beatitudes to the U.S. Constitution, they need to be reinterpreted as conditions change. But they still remain as fundamental clues for how best to begin building life together.

This sounds like and is a pitch for some very traditional work on the part of the church. Theology and ethics are the work of the church. They form the content of worship which occurs, quite properly, within the context of a variety of aesthetic expressions. They form the content of action whether that action is addressed to individuals or to the structures of society. Acknowledging that we are as caught in the identity crisis as anyone else, we too find that we are being driven back to our origins. But, in looking at the rock from which we were hewn, we must not fall into the idolatry of archaism.[3] We cannot turn the clock back, we cannot reinstate some romanticized, idealized pristine past. That kind of cursing the day we were born is a subtle blaspheming which blinds us to the God who is setting things right in the present, with or without us, often in manners never before experienced. The results can be as upsetting to the pious occultist as to the pious pew-warmer. The former has to deal with the thrust and reality of technology and corporate structure; the latter may have to get over a slavish adoration or mystical fear of them in order to shake them and make them serve humankind.

When God begins setting things right, which is much more the biblical meaning and base of righteousness than goody-goody behavior, it is generally the case that the people resist. We prefer the familiar charms of household deities and domestic idols to the perforce threatening motions of the Creator of/in the universe. But just because it is the Creator of the universe at work in it, resistance is ultimately useless. People and things begin to tremble and shake. And here we are in a trembling and shaking universe wondering and arguing about who or what is doing it to us. Here we are in a universe of staggering immensity and richness which beckons for our embrace while we nickel-dime ourselves to death over the small change of political rhetoric and tiny aggrandizement games. When and as we can begin to comprehend that it is God who is our undoing, and who will indeed undo us if necessary, we may realize that it is our idols that are under attack. We may be enabled to sort out our ideologies, our fads, our principalities and powers, and begin to build a life in which we take each other's existence as seriously as we take our own. Such are the lineaments of a genuine spiritual quest; it is a most fully human pursuit.

1. Garrett Hardin, "The Tragedy of the Commons," *Science Magazine*, December 13, 1968.

2. Werner Heisenberg, *Philosophic Problems of Nuclear Science* (New York: Pantheon, 1952), p. 118.

3. Ronald Gregor Smith, *The New Man* (London: SCM Press, 1956), pp. 72ff.

RICHARD A. UNDERWOOD:

## A Script(ure): Jesus and Nicodemus

There was one of the Pharisees named Nicodemus, a member of the Jewish Council, who came
to Jesus by night. "Rabbi," he said, "we know that
you are a teacher sent by God; no one could perform these signs of yours unless God were with
him." Jesus answered, "In truth, in very truth I tell
you, unless a man has been born over again he
cannot see the kingdom of God." "But how is it
possible," said Nicodemus, "for a man to be born
when he is old? Can he enter his mother's womb a
second time and be born?" Jesus answered, "In
truth I tell you, no one can enter the kingdom of
God without being born from water and spirit.
Flesh can give birth only to flesh; it is spirit that
gives birth to spirit. You ought not to be astonished, then, when I tell you that you must be born
over again."

St. John 3:1–7, NEB

This encounter consummates the themes we
have dealt with previously. This consummation can be
seen in terms of the dialectical relation between rebirth
(metamorphosis and transformation) on the one hand, and
completion, on the other hand. In these two themes, in
fact, we have not only a clue to the dynamics of the quest
of the young, but also a profound insight into the genius of
*Christian* dynamics. This latter observation is not meant to
suggest that the motivation of the "spiritual quest" is consciously Christian: but it must be observed that of the
amalgam of cultic-mythic forms which has shaped Western culture, Christian dynamics have been traditionally,
though too theoretically, dominant. Perhaps what we are

observing in the "spiritual quest of the young" is evidence that the message has finally got through!

In any event: to interpret the meaning of the encounter between Jesus and Nicodemus in terms of the dialectical relation between rebirth and completion is to say that without rebirth there is no completion and without completion there is no rebirth. The question remains, however: What do rebirth and completion *mean?* In concluding these indirect speculations I would like to explore this question from three perspectives: (1) societal and anthropological; (2) psychological; (3) religious.

A most helpful interpretation on rebirth/completion from the *societal-anthropological perspective* is offered by Joseph Campbell.[1] Basically, the argument of his interpretation is this: proportionately, man's dependency period is longer than any other species (twelve to twenty years, though, as Campbell notes, Bernard Shaw specifies it as seventy years!). That is, man is born *incomplete,* and the function of society is to assist in his completion. Here Campbell quotes Adolf Portmann: "Man is the incomplete creature whose style of life is the historical process determined by a tradition." [2] In this context, Campbell interprets society as a "second womb": "Society, as a fostering organ is thus a kind of exterior 'second womb,' wherein the post-natal stages of man's long gestation— much longer than that of any other placental—are supported and defended." [3] In other words: the "first" womb, the universal gestation place of all human kind, takes care of the organism in a beautifully symbiotic way. But the *second* "womb" of society must nurture (with biological and psychological justifications) the organism into a position of relative self-sufficiency. The gestation period in the *first* womb is nine months; the gestation period in the "second womb" is twelve, twenty, thirty years, depending upon the complexity of the culture.

The issue now is this: How can one be delivered from the "second womb" [of society] in a state of good health as one was delivered from the "first womb"? If the organism is delivered from the "first womb" either too late or too soon, it encounters great risks. By the same token, if the organism leaves the "second womb" of society either too soon, or too late, or not at all, then it is likely to be deformed. This is the point, then, at which rebirth becomes crucial: *How* does one leave the "second womb" and complete his life? The "first womb" takes care of biological necessities and prepares the way for psychological development. The "second womb" takes care of both biological and socio-psychological necessities. Rebirth out of the "second womb" seems to be the issue at stake in the encounter of Jesus and Nicodemus. One can leave it either too early or too late. But leave it one must if he is to achieve completion.

This brings us to the second perspective: the *psychological interpretation* of rebirth.

If the "first womb" has worked, and if the "second womb" has worked, then the person has been brought to a point of realizing his own peculiar potential. In the context of Jungian psychology, this is to be seen as the process of individuation. That is, once one has been conformed to biological dynamics (the "first womb") and once one has been conformed to the requirements of the "second womb" (sociological dynamics), then *what* remains to be done? What remains is man's true completion. That is, he must become who he is, himself; he must be metamorphized into a recognition of his true self. Without this the human being does not, in the final analysis, advance beyond the instinctual organization of colonies of bees and ants. He remains tied to bio-social dynamics. But *with* the movement into a sense of his own uniqueness two things are accomplished: (1) man finally discovers, and therefore *completes,* himself; (2) *meaning* is created for the universal animate-inanimate background out of which man emerges.

This is spoken to, psychologically, most directly in the so-called individuation process of the psychology of C. G. Jung. By individuation, Jung means "in general": ". . . the process of forming and specializing the individual nature; in particular, it is the development of the psychological individual as a differentiated being from the general, collective psychology. Individuation, therefore, is a *process of differentiation,* having for its goal the development of the individual personality." [4] The possibility of individuation, in the human sense, is rooted in the peculiarly ambiguous nature of human consciousness. Jung speaks to this when he says, in another context, and very early in his career (in fact, in his doctoral dissertation published in 1902): "It is conceivable that the phenomena of double consciousness are simply new character formations, or attempts of the future personality to break through. . . ." [5]

What are we to make of this? I submit the following:

1. Individuation can be seen in terms of *completion:* that is, individuation, in Jung's sense, is to be seen as a movement out of the collective (both biological and sociological) into the unique (the individual, which Jung describes in *Psychological Types* as "unique-being").

2. For human beings (as distinct from crystals such as snowflakes, which appear in unique form without benefit of the peculiar form of human consciousness), the possibil-

ity of individuation is rooted in "the phenomenon of *double* consciousness": that is, consciousness of past necessity and consciousness of future possibility (and this should be seen in terms of our earlier description from Heidegger, namely, the "double lack of the no-more and the not-yet").

3. The encounter between Jesus and Nicodemus on the question of rebirth indicates a "double consciousness" in Nicodemus: he recognized "new character formations" in himself, but he could refer them only to the "first womb," not to the possibility of a *new* breaking through.

This brings us to the third perspective—the *religious perspective*—on the issue of rebirth and completion.

I have tried to suggest that Nicodemus' encounter with Jesus indicates a *biological* readiness to realize "new character formations" of which, however, Nicodemus was unconscious. Nevertheless, he persisted and was forced, in his conversation, to take account of Jesus' response. For our purposes, the following observations are in order:

1. Jesus, in calling Nicodemus to the elements of water and Spirit was saying, I suggest: "You have fulfilled your *dharma*." To put it another way, he was saying to Nicodemus: "You have met the requirements of the law, but you are not yet complete. That is, you are not yet an individual because you perceive yourself only in terms of collective dynamics—both biological and sociological."

2. Jesus was saying also, according to our interpretation here: "It is now time for you to rediscover the basic, fundamental, original elements out of which all that *is* comes —namely, water and Spirit (the proper combination of which generates the fire of consciousness which enables you to see the unconsciousness of earth which is your previous condition)."

In short, the encounter between Jesus and Nicodemus can be read as a call for Nicodemus to recover the original elements of himself—and this recovering or reentry into water and Spirit can be seen as the possibility of rebirth. Nicodemus' refusal can be read as saying: "I am not yet ready to leave my societal forms: as a second womb they still serve me well."

In conclusion: the "spiritual quest of the young" *can* be interpreted as a quest for rebirth and completion. The young who are questing seem to be saying, unlike Nicodemus: "The time has come for me to say, 'Now I must leave the established orders and become, through the process of rebirth, who I am.' "

1. Joseph Campbell, *The Flight of the Wild Gander: Explorations in the Mythological Dimension* (New York: Viking Press, 1969); see especially chap. II, "Bios and Mythos," pp. 43–59.

2. *Ibid.,* p. 52. The quotation is from an essay by Portmann entitled "Das Ursprungs Problem" in *Eranos-Jahrbuch 1947* (Zurich: Rhein-Verlag, 1948).

3. *Ibid.,* p. 53.

4. C. G. Jung, *Psychological Types or, The Process of Individuation* (New York: Pantheon Books, 1959), p. 561.

5. C. G. Jung, "On the Psychology of So-called Occult Phenomena" in Vol. I of the Collected Works, *Psychiatric Studies* (New York: Pantheon Books, 1957), p. 79. For an expanded interpretation of this statement relative to individuation, see Jolande Jacobi, *The Way of Individuation* (New York: Harcourt, Brace and World, 1967), pp. 12ff.

BETSY BRENNEMAN:

## L'Envoi

Closing oneself off on Block Island was extremely difficult, especially in early June when the sight, hearing, and touch of life is so good. Coming together to talk of spiritual quest revealed the beauty of the human mind and heart as well as the prejudices and personal motivations that propel us all. Often I did not say much. I did not feel we had come for theological debate and so I refused to speak a language that seemed irrelevant to the problem. Yet that was my judgment of irrelevance and I tried to remain open.

Sharing many hours of words, I was conscious that I was young. I sat in awe of the experience, intellect, and spirit exhibited before me and I constructed my idols and paradigms. When I felt I was needed, I spoke of the condition of man in his youth today, I argued for what I had come to believe, and I cooperated on points which puzzled me.

I grew on Block Island. A community tends to do that to me. Sharing and uniting are great adhesives, stabilizing new steps into dark rooms. We called ourselves a church and with a slight sense of irony, we traced the spirit of man with words. It often made me smile until late into the evening before our final session when I was terrorized by the feeling that we were killing the spirit by our pursuit. The incident crystallized for me my personal condition, the state of the conference and the abstractness of what we were attempting, so much so that I had to write of it sadly, fearfully. Emotionally I decided to read what I had written during the night at our final gathering. Neglecting all thoughts of propriety I felt I had to speak to what had happened in relation to what we had hoped to accomplish. I share here a part of what I had written:

I choked tonight and then I felt my "youthness," for I felt an alienation so pervasive and powerful that the feelings I had for all of you were those I imagine we have all known—the horrible rage against those who are "wiser" than you, those who are older, who used to be parents and are always those whom we love. . . . I thought how ironic it was that we were all sitting there really thinking we were getting somewhere when all that was happening was that you were reshuffling the decks of your beliefs so they could be applied with a little more fervor. . . . I didn't really think I could teach you anything this week, but now, I have at least one insight to offer. Not only will you not be able to aid, you will actually become a sealed lock in the individual human canals flowing toward the river Om if you apply in order to relate. . . . The fact that the phenomenon of the Jesus freaks spoke powerfully to me about this spiritual quest, that unlike drugs, astrology, and Zen this spiritual turn is deeply imbedded in our culture and our psyche *was* important . . . and yet you could not open yourselves to me, let alone the freaks because they "are aberrations and perversions" of your Christianity. . . . In your admirable desire to be relevant you frighten me more than apathy. . . . If you wish to graft what is important to you onto the young you confront, I wish you all the luck. . . . I do care that you exerted the imperialism you detest on me. I agree that you cannot get inside another's skin, but if you can't provide at least me with the acceptant space of which you talk so affirmatively and eloquently, I no longer hold any illusions that you will be able to provide it for anyone else . . . the old dichotomy between knowing and doing. I believe that your concern rests equally with both, yet, possibly because you are such experts of thought you have delineated the first only . . . but I think that your understanding-for-doing needs to be enlarged a little by this statement. . . .

I could not talk of spirit anymore. I had to let mine loose. So from everything that had made me feel what I was feeling, from SRA readers to Kent State to Jesus freaks I let my insides out. We had come around to doing that which I saw young people despising and rejecting as less than humanizing. We were intoxicated with the rhythm of analyze-apply, analyze-apply until reality was hopelessly distorted.

The "ad hoc Block Island church" listened intently and then responded sincerely, emotionally. My spirit was taken in and shared, we united, we communed, and shortly we had to start our goodbyes. As I said, I grew on Block Island. My ability to open became broader and stronger. A true church had responded successfully to one human spirit. It had reacted beautifully to one young seeker. We were searching for ways of relating to the larger spiritual quest of youth and, fortunately, we were forced into a quest of our own.

I have told you from where I came and where I have arrived. Finally, I must tell you that I traveled beyond Block Island to Maine and a home called, significantly, Thresholds. There, several nights after I had watched the island disappear in the ferry's wake, I heard Galway Kinnell's *Book of Nightmares* read aloud and the spiritual quest, the longing for God, the essence and religiosity of all people were expressed: "Can it ever be true—all bodies, one body, one light made of everyone's darkness together?"